Cambridge E

Elements in Shakespe[...]
edited by
W. B. Worthen
Barnard College

STOICISM AS PERFORMANCE IN
MUCH ADO ABOUT NOTHING

Acting Indifferently

Donovan Sherman
Seton Hall University, New Jersey

CAMBRIDGE
UNIVERSITY PRESS

CAMBRIDGE
UNIVERSITY PRESS

University Printing House, Cambridge CB2 8BS, United Kingdom

One Liberty Plaza, 20th Floor, New York, NY 10006, USA

477 Williamstown Road, Port Melbourne, VIC 3207, Australia

314–321, 3rd Floor, Plot 3, Splendor Forum, Jasola District Centre,
New Delhi – 110025, India

79 Anson Road, #06–04/06, Singapore 079906

Cambridge University Press is part of the University of Cambridge.

It furthers the University's mission by disseminating knowledge in the pursuit of
education, learning, and research at the highest international levels of excellence.

www.cambridge.org
Information on this title: www.cambridge.org/9781108707299
DOI: 10.1017/9781108751797

© Donovan Sherman 2019

This publication is in copyright. Subject to statutory exception
and to the provisions of relevant collective licensing agreements,
no reproduction of any part may take place without the written
permission of Cambridge University Press.

First published 2019

A catalogue record for this publication is available from the British Library.

ISBN 978-1-108-70729-9 Paperback
ISSN 2516-0117 (online)
ISSN 2516-0109 (print)

Cambridge University Press has no responsibility for the persistence or accuracy of
URLs for external or third-party internet websites referred to in this publication
and does not guarantee that any content on such websites is, or will remain,
accurate or appropriate.

Stoicism as Performance in *Much Ado About Nothing*

Acting Indifferently

Elements in Shakespeare Performance

DOI: 10.1017/9781108751797

First published online: August 2019

Donovan Sherman

Seton Hall University, New Jersey

Author for correspondence: donovan.sherman@shu.edu

ABSTRACT: This Element demonstrates how Shakespeare's *Much Ado About Nothing* models an understanding of the philosophy of Stoicism as performance, rather than as intellectual doctrine. To do this, it explores how, despite many early modern cultural institutions' suppression of Stoicism's theatrical capacity, a performative understanding lived on in one of the most influential texts of the era, Baldassare Castiglione's *The Book of the Courtier*, and that this performativity was itself inherited from one of Castiglione's sources, Cicero's *De Oratore*. Donovan Sherman concludes with a sustained reading of *Much Ado* to demonstrate how the play, in performance, itself acts as a Stoic exercise.

KEYWORDS: Stoicism, performance, Shakespeare, Renaissance studies, theatre

© Donovan Sherman 2019

ISBNs: 9781108707299 (PB), 9781108751797 (OC)

ISSNs: 2516-0117 (online), 2516-0109 (print)

Contents

1 Why Truth?

The "nothing" of *Much Ado About Nothing* can mean practically anything. While the title's cryptic accusative seems to brush off any scrutiny—as in the "nothing" of expressions like "Oh, it's nothing"—many critics have felt compelled to give it metaphysical resonance. In a particularly rhapsodic example, Harold Goddard launches into a thought exercise that he views as a natural step for "those who seek a deeper meaning in the title." For Goddard, this "nothing" prompts associations of possibility, perspective, and infinity:

> If I draw a circle on the sand or on a piece of paper, instantly the spatial universe is divided into two parts, the finite portion within the circle (or the sphere if we think of it in three dimensions) and the infinite remainder outside of it. Actuality and possibility have a similar relation. Actuality is what is within the circle. However immense it be conceived to be, beyond it extends not merely the infinite but the infinitely infinite realm of what might have been but was not, of what may be but it not. (271–72)

Nothingness, with its dual registers of absence and the infinite, affords Goddard a springboard for philosophical inquiry. Goddard's essay dwells on the play's Christian themes, but his fundamental concern is Platonic; deeper meanings, invisible to the eye, reside beneath the pageant of the material and perceivable world. This mode of "nothing," reminiscent of its abundant usage in *King Lear*, is more concerned with ontology than simply with skeptical weariness: rather than "Oh, it's nothing," Goddard seems to exclaim, as recognizing a long-lost friend: "Oh, it's *nothing*!" Readings in this vein gained popularity as Shakespeare scholarship turned away from the character criticism of the early nineteenth century and concerned itself more with language, meaning, and symbolism. In this shift, *Much Ado* provided a useful vessel for discovering profound inquiries into the nature of reality itself, as evinced by the German critic Hermann Ulrici's observation that Shakespeare, in writing his comedy, "rather seems to have drawn his ground-idea from a contemplation of the contrasts which human life presents between

the reality of outward objects, and the perceptions of the inward subject"
(289). The phenomenological contrast noted here, which presumes
a difference between the knowable, if subjective, sensations of interiority
and the objective, if unknowable, status of external life, signals the increasing
prominence of *knowledge* as a scholarly topos for the play. In a 1956 lecture, A.
P. Rossiter pinpoints "imperfect self-knowledge" as its comic heart (65), and
Ralph Berry, in a 1971 reading that trains its eye on the play's structure, still
foregrounds its central theme as the "knowledge" that differentiates between
levels of perceptual reality by proposing "that we conceive of the theme of
Much Ado as an exploration of the limits and methods of humanly-acquired
knowledge" (213). Similarly, Richard Henze notes how *Much Ado*'s deception
can produce the salutary effect of allowing its lovers to be "caught by the mere
truth" (198). The title's apparently light dismissal of "nothing" as simply
inconsequence, as folly, has increasingly been saddled with the ironic weight
of gnomic meaning—"nothing," in this interpretive tradition, indexes the
limits of our consciousness; it serves as a modernist signal of humankind's
incapacity to grapple with paradoxical infinities of potentiality and negativity.
We might say that criticism of *Much Ado* has proposed how knowledge—the
accumulation of what we believe to be facts—can never quite align with truth
—the absolute fact of the matter always beyond our grasp.

    In what follows, I offer an alternative to the assumptions that underpin
this tradition, assumptions rooted in an even deeper, more implicit critical
preoccupation that appears so self-evident as to seem absurd: that the truth
matters, that the discovery of the truth is of paramount importance. In this
sense I would like to return to the seemingly more simple interpretation of
the play's title, the raised eyebrow that Puckishly dismisses as inconsequen-
tial our interest in wanting to stack up our knowledge in the first place. This
kind of epistemological brush-off is succinctly put by Michel Foucault in
a 1984 interview when, while fielding questions about power and knowledge
from his eager interlocutors, he responds by asking "Why truth? Why are
we concerned with truth, and more so than with the care of self? And why
must the care of the self occur only through the concern for truth?" (Ethics
of Concern 37). These questions, on their face, have the ring of postmodern
caricature: *Who cares about the truth?* But a wider view of the context
surrounding Foucault's query gives us appropriate historical and theoretical

entry points for a discussion of *Much Ado*. As evinced by his invocation of the "care of the self," Foucault was at the time reading and thinking deeply about the ancient Stoics; the interview takes place amidst several long lecture series at the College de France on the topic. In the same year as the interview, Foucault published a book called *The Care of the Self*, though that work—part of his vast, multivolume, unfinished project on the history of sexuality—strips away many of the longer, ruminative, and speculative explorations of the Stoics that took place in the lectures. Those lectures, relieved of the teleological pressure of conforming his readings into a wider narrative that eventually lands in what he will call biopolitics, constitute a powerful set of interlocutors for considerations of Stoicism's influence.[1]

However, to paraphrase Foucault, we might ask: Why the Stoics? What do the Stoics have to do with *Much Ado*? A lot, as it turns out, and as I aim to demonstrate. The philosophy helps us recover the title's sense of radical indifference by critiquing the belief that the separation of actuality from deception—the focus of critical readings preoccupied with the relationship of knowledge to truth—can proceed without first understanding and fine-tuning the fitness of the consciousness that must undertake the act of

---

[1] Foucault is admittedly an overdetermined figure to invoke in any work of literary scholarship. His work has received powerful criticism from a legion of disciplines (history, philosophy, literature) that have found his conclusions reductive and evidence scant. To take an exemplary case, Pierre Hadot, in *Philosophy as a Way of Life*, finds much to admire in Foucault's work but identifies a glaring blind spot in his discussion in *The Care of the Self* of the Stoic attitude toward joy. Stoic joy is not to be found strictly in the self, Hadot elaborates; it "can be found in what Seneca calls 'perfect reason' (that is to say, in divine reason) since for him, human reason is nothing other than reason capable of being made perfect"; as a result, the joyous portion of one's self is fundamentally a "transcendent self" (*Philosophy* 207). The understanding of Stoicism in *Care of the Self* perpetuates a secularized and non-metaphysical version of the philosophy. It is because of Foucault's tendency to make such sweeping and thinly researched claims in his published work that I draw instead on his much more considered and nuanced readings of the Stoics in his lectures. For perhaps the paradigmatic criticism of Focuault, see Habermas 238–93; for a recent and provocative accusation of Foucault's complicity with neoliberalism, see Behrent and Zamora.

perception. The play makes much ado about the assumption that anyone in it has properly cultivated the powers of attentiveness needed to even begin discovering the truth of the matter. In other words, *Much Ado* repeatedly steers its focus away from a pursuit of knowledge in hopes of ascertaining the truth; instead, it keeps beckoning its characters and audience members to first train themselves to know how to interpret anything. My connection of Stoicism to *Much Ado* is not simply the discovery of this symmetry; it is not only that the play exemplifies Stoic ideas or acts as a case study of a larger set of ideas. I focus here on more significant points of engagement. The first is historical. Shakespeare's comedy preoccupies itself with florid displays of wit and lightly satirical manifestations of early modern courtier culture, two elements that share Stoic forbearers, though this connection is little noted. The precise witty maneuvers performed in the play, in fact, can be traced back from Castiglione's *The Book of the Courtier* (a noted influence on the play) to its classical predecessor, Cicero's *De Oratore*, which, slyly and implicitly, links rhetoric to Stoic ideals.

The play's second Stoic affinity is more abstract: it exists in its execution of what I am calling Stoic performance. "Performance" is an admittedly capacious term—the field of performance studies has applied it, at times perhaps too loosely, to objects of study as varied as professional sports, gender, animal behavior, video games, and even rock formations. While I am wary of employing an overly broad understanding of performance in my discussion of Stoicism and *Much Ado*, I do believe the philosophy earns this categorization for its situation as neither textually doctrinal nor aesthetically theatrical. To be a Stoic was to *behave* in a certain way, to practice what Pierre Hadot, a contemporary philosopher and scholar of early antiquity, calls a "way of life." As the Stoic philosopher Epictetus puts it, in a favorite passage of Hadot's, a "carpenter does not come up to you and say 'Listen to me discourse about the art of carpentry,' but he makes a contract for a house and builds it" (qtd. in *Philosophy* 91). A Stoic does not talk about philosophy; a Stoic *lives* in a philosophical manner. The Stoics explained how one had to repeatedly adhere to a program of exercise, known as *askesis*, to promote existence in the continuous present. The habitual execution of these exercises, which ranged from imagining one's death to noting the passage of emotions and sensations one could feel to witnessing the willed destruction of seemingly necessary aspects of life—trains individuals to be aware, to follow reason, and to evaluate and understand sensations and emotions. These elements bind Stoicism to a broad grammar of performance, not as a formalist set of principles (there is no Stoic equivalent of Aristotle's *Poetics*) but as what Richard Schechner has memorably termed "twice-behaved, coded, transmittable behaviors": restored and restorable, even ritualistic, executions of intentional actions (52). This notion of performance has rendered porous the boundaries of staged work and everyday life, and the paradigmatic work of performance theorists such as Joseph Roach, Peggy Phelan, and Diana Taylor has allowed for more catholic understandings of "theatre" that link the rehearsed and performed work of the stage to the rehearsed and performed work of politics, culture, and identity.

In drawing out connections between Shakespeare's drama and performance theory, I align myself with the work of scholars such as Erika T. Lin, Andrew Sofer, and Miles P. Grier, and perhaps most clearly with the foundational work of William B. Worthen.[2] The interdisciplinary interventions of these thinkers have carved out new interpretive paradigms for reading early modern texts as not simply static, archival signals of historical or literary import but also as inextricably linked to embodiment—and not just the predetermined embodiment of their staging. The burgeoning subfield of Shakespeare performance studies allows for the drama to present, not simply re-present, the material and bodily grammar of off-stage performances such as religious ritual, civic festival, and even the enactment of gendered and racial identity. As Grier puts it, in a study of an early American production of *Macbeth*, a broader sense of early modern "performance culture"—not simply the staged production, limned by the walls of the theatre building—"mediated perceptions of real events" (78). That is,

---

[2] The intersection of performance studies and Shakespeare studies contains multitudes: scholars such as Franklin J. Hildy devote themselves to the accurate reconstruction of the "original practices" of Shakespeare's theatrical art; on the other hand, more theoretical approaches may read Shakespeare's drama as meditations on the nature *of* performance—as works of performance theory themselves. For a bracing example of this latter case, see Sofer 28–65.

the "real" performances that constitute habituated life find their extension, not fictive separation, on the Shakespearean stage, and likewise, staged Shakespearean works structure the perception of "real" events. Seen this way, Stoic exercises certainly constitute a mode of behavior that can be linked to the formal enactment of drama, as they provide a type of performance that, on its face, resists categorization as either entirely theatrical or experiential. Stoicism was between the two Platonic poles of the aleatory, non-repeatable events of life and the artistic, iterable imitation of it.[3] It was neither the raw material of the represented nor the refined simulacra of the representative; Stoic activity lived in a space between drama and spontaneity. It was a practice, and thus a type of performance, and while it was not strictly theatre, it certainly could (and, I will argue, did) infiltrate the theatre.

The goal of the performance of *askesis* is to focus only on what one can control: one's capacity for reason, which in turn allows the realization of a virtuous life. To everything else, the Stoic must profess indifference (*apatheia*), a word activated as both the philosopher's disposition and the *adiaphora*, or "things indifferent," which the Stoic was unconcerned with differentiating. Hadot, in an inspired passage of his book *Philosophy as a Way of Life*, plays with this double meaning when he claims that the task of Stoicism is to educate people to know only "the goods they are able to obtain" and to know the difference between good and evil:

> In order for something good to be always obtainable, or an evil always avoidable, they must depend exclusively on man's freedom; but the only things which fulfil these conditions are *moral* good and evil. They alone depend on us; everything else does *not* depend on us. Here, "everything

---

[3] Paul Kottman has explored how even this seemingly reified boundary between Platonic *mimesis* and the affective immediacy of "actual" emotion may be blurred. In an essay on Herodotus' account of Phrynichus' tragedy *The Fall of Miletus*, Kottman takes up Hannah Arendt's claim that the theatre is "pre-philosophical" to account for how the actuality of mourning can infiltrate its attempted representation (83).

else," which does not depend on us, refers to the necessary
linkage of cause and effect, which is not subject to our
freedom. It must be indifferent to us: that is, we must not
introduce any differences into it, but accept it in its entirety,
as willed by fate. This is the domain of nature. (*Philosophy*
83, italics in original)

To be a Stoic, for Hadot, is to practice the dictum with which Epictetus
begins his *Enchiridion*: "Some things are up to us and some things are not
up to us" (*Handbook*, 11). Epictetus' limpid proclamation finds moral
resonance in the performative day-to-day and moment-to-moment
upkeep of attentiveness needed to separate contingent things from
Hadot's "everything else," the domain of nature that need not invite our
curiosity, much less mastery, and need not have differences introduced. It
is indifferent to us and we resist layering differences upon it. This is the
form of indifference that *Much Ado* urges us to comport ourselves with
when evaluating knowledge. Rather than see a gap in our knowledge,
however, or rather than pursue the truth through the fallible medium of
our human understanding, the Stoic exercise of Shakespeare's play—what
it *does*, not what it *means*—invites an embodied refocus onto our own
selves. To ground this distinction briefly in an example from the play:
rather than care about the "truth" of a situation (Claudio does not realize
that it is Ursula, not Hero, whom he witnesses with a lover) the Stoic
would question whether the perceived circumstances stem from reason or
not. Did Claudio adequately train himself to be attentive to which
cognitive and affective inputs correlate to reason?

In focusing on Stoicism's performative dimension, I differ from
literary scholars who have largely studied the classical philosophy's
intellectual inheritance. To be sure, the foundational work by T.S.
Eliot, Gordon Braden, Andrew Shifflet, Reid Barbour, Patrick Gray,
and others has helped trace vital connections between early modern
poetry and drama and early modern translations and adaptations of
texts by figures such as Marcus Aurelius, Epictetus, and, most promi-
nently, Seneca, alongside the Neo-Stoic work of Justus Lipsius. But the
study of Stoicism as a set of doctrines and ideas that wind their way

through early modern culture—surfacing, say, as *sententiae* and aphorisms in grammar instruction books and manuals of political and legal conduct, or as portentous speechifying in Senecan tragedies—elides the philosophy's inheritance as a performed way of life, one that often opposed itself to precisely the sagacious-seeming nuggets of wisdom that characterize Stoicism's more doctrinal disseminations. Thus while I agree with Braden that early modern Stoicism constitutes not a "set of static norms" but "an ongoing process of reinterpretation and revision" (3), I do not limit this organic quality to the text, but instead see texts as principles of embodied, practical living, not as bound maps of conceptual terrain. It is thus contemporary Stoic philosophers and critics such as Foucault, Hadot, and Martha Nussbaum who provide my major interlocutors, as their readings of Stoicism remain alive to the possibility of the philosophy's vital and lived-in qualities.

The difference between Stoicism as a set of principles to know, on the one hand, and Stoicism as an embodied performance to learn, on the other, helps illuminate why I can search for its existence in a play such as *Much Ado* even though it explicitly professes distaste for the philosophy. In perhaps the most florid gesture of Stoicism's apparent rejection, Leonato, in the throes of false mourning for his daughter, Hero, waves away consolation with a dismissal of philosophy's efficacy:

> I pray thee peace; I will be flesh and blood.
> For there was never yet philosopher
> That could endure the toothache patiently,
> However they have writ the style of gods
> And make a push at chance and sufferance.

(5.1.34–38)

Although not named, the particular philosophy that Leonato takes aim at is clearly Stoicism, and his overdrawn picture of Stoicism as stuffy misanthropy survives in its small-s terminology today: to be "stoic" often denotes an unhealthy denial of feeling. Leonato's lines rehearse the early modern origins of this commonplace, which features in many dramatic scenes of the era that reject philosophy as a comically inadequate salve for the real feelings and sensations of life. This was not an inaccurate picture, provided our understanding of the philosophy limited itself to adages, ideas, and other digestible sentiments and not the performed engagement encouraged by its classical sources. Perhaps most emblematically, the trope of rejecting Stoicism appears in Hamlet's rebuttal to his former schoolmate: "There are more things in heaven and earth, Horatio, / Than are dreamt of in your philosophy" (1.5.174–75). Leonato elevates Hamlet's claim to high dudgeon. Stoics, Leonato claims, cannot account for the realities of "flesh and blood." In fact, they can barely handle a toothache, a telling choice of ailment, as Benedick's toothache has already served as a symptom of romantic attraction. Write all the lovely words you want, Leonato implies: when faced with pain and love, abstract beliefs collapse.

In early modern dramaturgy, Stoics often serve as foils for the more kinetic and full-blooded actions of a comic or tragic protagonist. To take a particularly self-aware example, Ben Jonson's *Bartholomew Faire* playfully calls attention to the archetypal Stoic figure when Adam Overdo, a justice of the peace, finds himself humiliatingly strapped into the stocks at the titular celebration. When asked if he sighs or groans or "rejoice[s] in his affliction," he responds "I do not feel it, I do not think of it, it is a thing without me" before reciting some lines of Horace in Latin (4.6.91–94). Another observer exclaims "What's here? A stoic i'the stocks? The fool is turned philosopher" (4.6.100–1). The stock Stoic finds himself in actual stocks that physically manifest the paralysis associated with his philosophy. Overdo, despite his name, is more notable here for what he does *not* do: unfeeling and unthinking, he finds comfort in the kind of textual therapy at which Leonato sneers.

But the form of Stoicism that Leonato mocks and Overdo satirically emblematizes is one realized textually, rather than in the performed way of life celebrated by Hadot and the coy deferment of truth effected by Foucault. It is, in other words, the flattened and overly intellectual version too often conflated with the more vital understanding. Hence, in *Much Ado*, the frequent distaste for philosophy is always a distaste for philosophy that founds itself in words, in language. Moments before his stock dismissal of stock Stoicism, Leonato had railed against those who would, Overdo-like, "patch grief with proverbs" (5.1.34–38). In a more minor key, *Much Ado* frequently satirizes as inefficient the "paper bullets" that litter its plot with witticisms and idioms. "Dost thou think I care for satire or an epigram?" asks Benedick at the close, in an apparent show of his redeemed belief in the virtue of dealing with emotional realities head-on (5.4.99). And Don John, wallowing in his melancholy, acts offended at the consolation of philosophy proffered by Borachio: "I wonder that thou—being as thou sayst thou art, born under Saturn—goest about to apply a moral medicine to a mortifying mischief" (1.3.10–12). Borachio has simply advised that Don John "hear reason," but even this misapprehends how reason figured itself philosophically; rather than something heard (merely a word, a phrase, a sentence), reason was something done, something practiced.

While the play continually disavows the possibility of philosophy resolving itself into transmittable and communicable language, it does realize Stoicism's practiced incarnation as *askesis*. It does so in its repeated gestures of reorienting the audience and its characters away from placing a premium on the accumulation of knowledge in pursuit of the truth—away from chasing the "nothing" that tempts us with the promise of the infinite—and instead leveling its gaze on the faculties of the self that would embark on such a journey. The Stoic needed to examine deeply their own ability to perceive before they could even begin to care definitively about what is real or not, and *Much Ado* performs the training needed to undertake this examination more than it does the actual examination. It thus realizes in dramatic performance a mode of practice—that is, it aestheticizes and theatricalizes a type of performance meant to be executed in the space of one's private life. To explore this process further, my task here is threefold. I want to introduce Stoicism as a way of life that professes kinship to contemporary understandings of performance. I want to demonstrate how that way of life lived on in the early modern era despite efforts to reduce it to intellectual platitudes. And I want to show that *Much Ado* has historical, theoretical, and practiced resonances with this mode of performance. Before arriving at a sustained reading of *Much Ado*, then, I will need to explore thoroughly different forms of Stoicism at length; this lengthy digression is necessary in order to counter the persistent narrative of Stoicism as intellectual knowledge by tracing the long story of the philosophy's mode of embodiment winding its way from exercises in ancient Athens to banter in Shakespearean comedy.

2 Why Representation?

Stoicism thrives on practice. In his *Letters on Ethics* Seneca explains that "philosophy teaches us to act, not to speak" (20.2). But all that remains of the original Stoics are words. Recovering the performance of Stoicism relies on reconstructing embodied engagement out of the textual medium that the philosophy actively resists. The archive of Stoicism, in the early modern era as well as today, consists primarily of Marcus Aurelius' *Meditations*, Epictetus' *Enchiridion*, and the essayistic work of Seneca. (Secondhand reflections on Stoicism have survived in Diogenes Laertius' *Lives and Opinions of Eminent Philosophers*, Galen's *On the Views of Hippocrates and Plato*, and in commonplace books such as Aulus Gellius' *Attic Nights*.) Readers searching these works eager for a clear and systematic understanding of the philosophy will be disappointed, as they lack any clear program for behavior and instead comprise an artifact of a lost practice, a trace of performative behavior rather than an intellectually digestible overview. Marcus Aurelius' *Meditations* catalogues the emperor's daily routine of mental and physical activity, with entries that provide prompts for his behavior rather than any cohesive conclusions. His book was meant only to be a private diary rather than anything more widely applicable. Epictetus' *Enchiridion*, alternately called *The Handbook*, consists of transcriptions of his commentary made by his student Arrian, who recorded Epictetus' informal conversations after his lectures. And Seneca's works, while meant for wider consumption, still refuse clear-cut adaptation into scholastic models, instead offering freewheeling and digressive conversations about a range of often trivial issues. These texts are both residue of and prompt for embodied action and are thus necessarily insufficient components of a wider performative grammar. To read Stoic instructions does not give a complete picture of a philosophy, any more than reading the instruction manual for assembling a table would give you a table, or reading Yoko Ono's text for *Cut Piece*, her foundational work of Fluxus performance, gives us a sense of her art. (Ono's text reads, in its entirety, "Cut.")

The pupil who reads Stoic philosophy is meant to interact with the text as they would a person. Martha Nussbaum compares this behavior to the "critical spectatorship" called for by Bertolt Brecht because "the main aim" of Stoic advice "must be to create a spectator who is vigilant and probing, active rather than receptive" ("Poetry and the Passions" 138).[4] This vigilant spectatorship should then be carried forth into life, just as Brecht's dispassionate viewer leaves the theatre and remains critical of the theatrical illusions in civil society. The Stoic reader must complete the embodied act of reading by reflecting, thinking, and doing; hence the Stoics' frequent use of the exhortative mode as signal of the insufficiency of writing. As Hadot writes,

> The philosophical act is not situated merely on the cognitive level, but on that of the self and of being. It is a progress which causes us to *be* more fully, and makes us better. It is a conversion which turns our entire life upside down, changing the life of the person who goes through it. It raises the individual from an inauthentic condition of life, darkened by unconsciousness and harassed by worry, to an authentic state of life, in which he attains self-consciousness, an exact vision of the world, inner peace, and freedom. (*Philosophy* 83)

---

[4] The theatrical theories and innovations of Brecht are too numerous to list here, but insofar as Nussbaum explains his fundamental notion of "distancing," she evokes his groundbreaking manifesto on how theatre must produce critical spectators capable of reflecting on the mutability of the world around them, and it must do so through foregrounding the artifice of the stage and disavowing the dominance of the Aristotelian dependency on emotional cathexis. As Brecht puts it, in order to produce *verfremdungseffekts* (often translated awkwardly into English as "A-effects," or "alienation-effects"), "the actor has to discard whatever means he has learnt of getting the audience to identify itself with the characters which he plays" (193).

It is the philosophical *act* that constitutes philosophy, not that which might take place on the "cognitive level." This is a pre-Cartesian conception of wisdom shot through with a pre-modern embrace of morality: there is good, and bad, and philosophy helps us become better by knowing which is which. Such language may sound simplistic to our contemporary ears, but its implications possess more complexity than suggested by the invocation of a binary sense of right and wrong. The key to unlocking this complexity lies in an understanding of virtue, a key term that informs Hadot's focus on living an "authentic" life. Stoic virtue is not, as the term is often used today, a referendum on the moral implications of our behavior. William Irvine makes the case with clarity by noting that Stoic virtue, for a hypothetical acolyte, "depends on her excellence as a human being—on how well she performs the function for which humans were designed ... a virtuous individual is one who perform well the function for which humans were designed" (35–36). This principle originated with one of the original Greek Stoics, Zeno, who reportedly asked that we live in accordance to nature. The authenticity Hadot calls for springs from this alignment, as does the elevation of attention (*prosoche*) as one of the key components of Stoic practice. "Attention to the present moment," Hadot claims, "is, in a sense, the key to spiritual exercises" (*Philosophy* 84). Attentiveness allows for adjustments needed to maintain attunement to nature.

Articulating the aim of this attentiveness proves difficult to the aspiring Stoic because it unyokes itself from a straightforward investment in knowledge. Philosophers frequently focus on how to achieve virtue rather than what virtue is, and this circuitousness paradoxically comprises a Stoic goal. To perform in a way consonant with nature is to examine rigorously how we can do so. It is not to presume that we know what that might bring us, for that would wrench us out of the present and reroute our attention onto something indifferent, in the classical sense: something contingent, not dependent on our actions. Epictetus would ask us to cleave such concerns away from the focus of our attention. Marcus Aurelius, a close reader of Epictetus, adapts this circularity into daily practice in the self-examinations of his *Meditations*:

> What does happiness consist of? It consists of doing that
> which the nature of mankind desires. How shall we do this?

> By possessing those dogmas which are the principles of impulses and of action. Which dogmas? Those which pertain to the distinction of what is good from what is bad. There is no good for mankind but that which renders him just, temperate, courageous and free, and there is no evil for mankind, except that which brings about in him the contrary vices. (qtd. in Hadot, *Citadel* 37)

The pattern of repeated inquiries suggests a Socratic interest in discovering first principles. But instead of following a Platonic model, which would provoke the discovery, through the accretion of knowledge, of a fundamental metaphysical truth behind the appearances of life, these questions lead Marcus Aurelius back to where he began. He asks what happiness consists of and ends by claiming that goodness makes him happy, and that he must always make the "distinction" between good and bad. As conclusions go, this is unsatisfying from a standpoint of scholastic inquiry because it contains no knowledge that benefits the reader. Instead, the reading itself supplies the benefits of the practice. Marcus Aurelius reminds himself to focus on goodness in his actions and to link those actions only to values that promote goodness. The nature and goal of the actions themselves remain opaque, and instead we double back continuously to questioning the quality of attentiveness that allows for parsing out good from bad.

Marcus Aurelius' meditation encapsulates key differences between Stoicism and similar-seeming classical philosophies, such as Epicureanism, Skepticism, or Cynicism. First, Stoicism advocates for the complete eradiation of the passions, rather than their moderation or suppression. Second, it believes in a single-minded pursuit of reason, and a sole reasoning function of the soul, instead of accommodating non-reasoning elements, such as the Platonic and Aristotelian conceptions of vegetative and sensual components of the soul. Third, and as a result of the first two beliefs, Stoicism holds that the passions had to stem from one's ability to reason. The passions were bad judgments, not emotions. As Chrysippus, one of the early Greek Stoics, puts it, passions are "false judgment or false belief" (qtd. in Nussbaum, *Therapy*

366). To judge is to succeed or fail in accurately surmising the truth of something, or as Nussbaum puts it, "judgment, for the Stoics, is defined as an assent to an appearance" (*Therapy* 374). What Stoic practice must attend to vigilantly is the way by which the soul can practice correct judgment by studying if and how one assented to an appearance.

As exemplified by Marcus Aurelius' repeated turns to his own consciousness, the process by which the passions must be eliminated focuses inward, not outward, to train scrutiny on the proper ability to discern right from wrong so as to groom out the poor judgments of the passions. The elimination of the passions, then, arrives not via witnessing, in an Aristotelian moment of catharsis, the synchronized *anagnorisis* and *peripeteia* of a character in an imitation of action. *Pace* Aristotle, one did not attach to and identity with external manifestations so as to rid oneself of pity and fear. Instead, the Stoic sought to correct incorrect judgments by healing the capacity to reason—by applying philosophy as if it were medicine for the sense. This cure orients itself inward, not outward, and it depends on reason, the very aspect of the soul that it sought to fix. Nussbaum elaborates this idea syllogistically:

> If passions are not subrational stirrings coming from our animal nature, but modifications of the rational faculty, then, to be moderated and eventually cured they must be approached by a therapeutic technique that uses the arts of reason. And if judgments are all that the passions are, if there is no part of them that lies outside the rational faculty, then a rational art that sufficiently modifies judgments, seeking out the correct ones and installing them in place of the false, will actually be sufficient. (*Therapy* 367)

It is the totalizing quality of this prescription that further sets Stoicism apart from its rival classical philosophies. The passions are not to be wrestled with, as in Cynicism, nor offset with their opposite, as with Skepticism, but eliminated, root and branch, from the self. And because the passions originate from the reasoning faculty, they must themselves be treated with reason.

We can see a set of dualities emerging. Stoicism is not cognitive, but it focuses inward; it trains its practice only on reason, but it depends on action. From these dualities one can see the beginnings of the bloodless stereotype of the Stoic that eventually gains definition in the early modern era. To possess no passions is to be capable of only clear-eyed reason, capable of constant attentiveness to know how one can always follow reason to reach the full capacity of the self and thus live the good life and be virtuous. So far, this sounds like the killjoy sneered at by Leonato. But we can also detect a nascent theatrical quality missing from Stoicism's early modern invocations. The original Stoics, after all, did not profess any outright hostility to the theatre; in fact, they turned to it as a helpful model for their prescribed mode of being. As Epictetus puts it to his reader in *Enchiridion*, "Remember that thou art an actor in a play of such a kind as the teacher may choose; if short, of a short one, if long, of a long one" (*Handbook* 16). In a passage of his *Discourses*, Epictetus offers advice to a friend who has acted improperly while watching a comic play: "You ought then to know when you enter the theatre that you enter as a rule and example to the rest how they ought to look at the acting" (*Discourses* 204). These appeals urge the potential philosopher to think of themselves always in full view, as if on a stage, even when in the audience of an actual play. This Stoic mode of theatricality relies on theatrical attentiveness, but when coupled with its liberation from Aristotle's insistence on catharsis and Plato's focus on forms, its prescribed scrutiny, like Marcus Aurelius' circular meditation, sidesteps any metaphysical payoff. There is not a concern for attaining a sense of absolute truth through the investigation of our knowledge; there is no ascent out of the cave. Attention to the self allows for a closer look at—the self.

A cool-headed, utterly reasonable figure who gazes at herself without emotions or curiosity in deeper truths: here again lie the roots of the comically unfeeling Stoic who shrugs off suffering. What becomes clear in a closer examination of classical Stoic works, however, is that this figure is an *ideal*, that it is nearly impossible to attain a state of truly removing the passions. It is true that the Stoic sage—the figure who has completely eliminated all attachments to contingent things, who has perfected a sense of reason through constant attention—does not succumb to inaccurate representations through poor judgments. As Irvine explains, though, this sage is nearly mythical and strategically framed as such. The Stoics "talk about sages primarily so they will have a model to guide them in their practice of Stoicism. The sage is a target for them to aim at, even though they will probably fail to hit it" (37).[5] Most Stoics were by definition *aspiring* Stoics, and the actions needed to realize their philosophy made them feel the very passions they sought to remove. Nussbaum, after closely reading what she calls "wonderful phenomenological descriptions" of the early Stoics, clarifies this point. The various accounts of attempts to uproot the passions "show us that the Stoics are not neglecting the way passions feel. What they insist is that, in each case, the thing feels like this is an act of assent or acknowledgment. Some recognitions feel like embracing a nail; others like rubbing yourself across a rough, grating surface; other propositions 'cut' differently, so other acceptances have a different phenomenological content" (*Therapy* 387). To practice is to acknowledge, and to acknowledge is to possess a feeling. Thus the Stoic must experience the physical sensations symptomatic of poor judgments as they are extirpated from the soul. This quality of emotion, of affect, disappears when the Stoic of the early modern era appears as a viable stock character, but even into late antiquity, Stoicism's potential to manifest as the struggle of the soul's interaction with emotions remained. Harold Attridge explains, in an essay on Stoic influences on early Christianity, that followers of Stoicism "may experience the emotional tug, the 'irrational contraction,' but will respond to it with some therapy, an alternative impression, an argument perhaps, convincing themselves that the proposition embedded in or implied by the 'contraction' is wrong" (84). Stoics focus on the elimination of poor judgments and their attendant emotions but they feel the sensations that arise during this process. It is again instructive to think of Stoicism as a performance, to grant philosophy a temporal axis on which to see its continual practice rather than short-cut a way to its neat epigrammatic conclusions.

Stoic *askesis* can last a lifetime and most likely will end in failure, but this failure designates an ironic feature of the practice as it brings the philosopher closer to, not further from, a greater sense of embodied humanity. The

---

[5] For a nuanced recovery of the sage as not simply a cerebral ideal but also capable of valuing materiality, see Dealy.

Stoics hold that, in Nussbaum's words, "life, if we attach ourselves to it, alienates us from our own humanity" (*Therapy* 421). This paradox is worth sitting with: Humanity exists not in the dialectical relationship of consciousness with the external world, nor the testing of representations for truth, but instead in the lived sensation of attempting to discover the self by fine-tuning a capacity for reason. The only way to do this is to act with the integrity born from rigorous self-examination so as to create a philosophical way of life. The creation of the disposition that can properly absorb reason, not the reason itself, is the end goal. So unknown is the wider structure of the world (the "author" whose intentions Epictetus shrugs off) that we waste our time and distance ourselves from our humanity if we focus on it. Instead we look inward, and the looking is the process *and* the product.

For Foucault, a distinct feature of this beguilingly circular nature is that it allows for neither purely philosophical nor spiritual claims to result. Stoic practice, for Foucault, cannot be reduced merely to intellectual axioms or doctrine. In *The Hermeneutics of the Subject*, a collection of his lectures at the Collège de France that center in large part on Stoicism, Foucault labels "philosophy" the discourse that "determines that there is and can be truth and falsehood and whether or not we can separate the true and the false," whereas "we could call 'spirituality' the search, practice, and experience through which the subject carries out the necessary transformations on himself in order to have access to the truth." The difference is one of the subject's transformation as a result of accessing the truth, as spiritual practices are those "which are, not for knowledge but for the subject, for the subject's very being, the price to be paid for access to the truth" (*Hermeneutics* 15). For Foucault, the Stoics are at a midpoint of these two modes. Stoic practice does not concern itself with questions of accessing the truth, but neither does it seek to refute the subject's identity.[6] Like Epictetus' imagined theatre, it lives only in the captivation of the here and now; it presents only itself.

---

[6] The Christian imperative to be reborn hinges on a death; see especially the epistles of Saint Paul ("And you hath he quickened, who were dead in trespasses and sins" from Ephesians 2:1, for example) and the growing body of Pauline criticism of Shakespeare and early modernity (Kuzner, Lupton, Eskew).

Later in *The Hermeneutics of the Subject*, in a discussion of Seneca's *Letters on Ethics*, Foucault observes that in Letter 65, where Seneca exhorts his friend Lucilius to examine the world around him, "there is no question of the soul withdrawing into itself and questioning itself in order to discover within itself the memory of the pure forms it had once seen. Rather, what is involved is really seeing the things of the world, of really grasping their details and organization" (*Hermeneutics* 281).

The conclusion Seneca urges Lucilius to reach in Letter 65 is humble. It resolves into neither the transformative recollection of *anamnesis* nor the self-abnegating force of religious conversion. Seneca acknowledges the transcendence of the truth but forecloses on the possibility of that transcendence transforming the subject. Lucilius need only focus on one element, reason, both within him and in the world, because, as Seneca puts it, everything has a cause, and that cause is reason (*Letters* 65.2). Like Marcus Aurelius' meditation, distinction supplies its own end: We distinguish by-products of our reason from contingent things, things indifferent, and cultivate the attentiveness characteristic of spiritual exercise. Nussbaum explains that if we are not ever-vigilant in ascertaining reason's role in the universe, we may "confuse the *instrumenta*—for example, wealth and status —with that life itself" (*Therapy* 356). Seneca's process of examination, then, may appear to be outward-facing, but in fact the primary site of his practice is the same as Marcus Aurelius': the interior subject. The Stoic refocuses inward the energy otherwise spent on the metaphysical possibilities of externalities, which results in an ethical tradeoff. "If declaring worldly activity external and unnecessary eases the agent's ethical burden in one way," claims Nussbaum, "in another way it increases it, by focusing all ethical attention on the internal doings of the heart" (364).[7]

---

[7] Early modern adaptations of Stoicism similarly emphasized a dismissal of ephemeral things. As Justus Lipsius dramatically exclaims in *De Constantia*, his Christianized gloss of a Senecan exchange, "Seest thou the Sun? He fainteth. The Moone? She laboureth and languisheth. The Starres? They faile and fall. And however the wit of man cloaketh and excuseth these matters, yet there have happened and daily do in that celestiall bodie such things as confound both the rules and the wittes of Mathematicians" (35).

Foucault pushes his conclusions further than Nussbaum or Hadot. Stoicism, for Foucault, represents the embryonic version of the self-care regimes that would eventually lead to the biopolitical operations of the state.[8] But Stoicism also contains a refreshing rejection of one of the basic assumptions of Western metaphysics: a pursuit of truth, a concern over the integrity of our knowledge. As such, Stoicism, while linked genealogically to the disciplinary modes Foucault famously explores elsewhere, also presents a radical undoing of civilization's aims when taken on its own terms and divorced from typology. This is the excitement underpinning his question "Why truth?" In a 1981 lecture, Foucault hints at the liberating possibilities of this line of thinking. After a long section of closely reading manuals of marriage and proper sexual conduct, Foucault notes that Stoic exercises result in no "developed relationship of knowledge" and have "nothing like those subtle and suspicious decipherments that will be found, for example, in Christians with regard to the flesh." He does allow the faint premonition of the nearly pathological focus on corporeality that, in his telling, Christian morality inaugurates. While not a site of knowledge production, the Stoic practices of the self contain a "kernel, the primordial and elementary form of a relationship of self to self that is at the same time a relationship of obectivation" (*Subjectivity* 285). The Stoics etch the bare outline of a relationship one has to one's own body by staking out the more elemental relationship of self to self, the very connection Seneca urges Lucilius to take up in his practice.

Foucault's readings help us add a political resonance to the non-Platonic and non-Aristotelian grammar of performance that coalesces around Stoicism. To behave in a Stoic manner is not to concern oneself with the truth of forms or even with the possibility of representation; it is not to follow the genealogies of mimesis that dominate considerations of Western theatre. It is instead to embody self-scrutiny as a continuous process that supplies its own end, to profess and corporeally effect total indifference toward that which *is* indifferent; it is instead to view life as a constant

---

[8] For an overview of the field of biopolitics as derived from Foucault, see Campbell and Sitze. For an exemplary discussion of biopolitics and early modern drama, see Leo.

theatrical enactment—not the *theatrum mundi* that analogizes character as social role, but as a pressurizing force that sharpens one's faculties of discernment. By denying the importance of Plato's epistemology, Stoicism creates a form of performance that resists cooption into the systems of power that depend on the creation of knowledge.

In its focus on interior virtue and disregard of authenticity, the Stoic mindset seems somehow both antiquated and vulgarly post-structuralist. Shakespeare's *Much Ado About Nothing* is instructive here in its recuperation of Stoicism as a vital practice. *Much Ado* is concerned, even obsessed, with examining different scenes of inter-action and evaluating their content. We might, like scholars in the crucial tradition who follow the ontological promise of "nothing," be tempted to think that such evaluations hinge on questions of evaluat-ing knowledge in terms of its proximity to truth (do characters "really" see what they think they see?) and connect this pattern to the play's interest in acting and theatricality. After all, it appears obvious to say that *Much Ado* consists of a series of scenes in which characters do not know what they need to know and that the play proceeds by revealing, at times with a perverse slowness abetted by misapprehension, the "truth" of the situations held at bay: Don John orchestrates the scene that Claudio mistakes for Hero's seduction; Benedick and Beatrice are not aware of each other's, or their own, romantic feelings.

But the play continually shifts its focus away from concerns for the truth and instead tracks the ways in which the characters *prepare* themselves for the truth to arrive. Seneca, in Letter 108, anticipates the kind of dramatic criticism practiced by readers who discover a "theme" of knowledge, self- or otherwise. After citing a passage of Virgil ("The best times of our lives, poor mortal creatures, / first fly away") Seneca asks Lucilius to consider different ways one could approach an understanding of the text.

> The one who reads with the eye of a literary scholar does not consider why the best times of our lives come first—that in their place comes illness, that old age looms over us even while we are still intent on our youth. Instead, he says that

> Virgil always uses the words "illness" and "old age"
> together. So he does, and with good reason! For old age is
> an illness that has no cure. (*Letters* 108.28)

Later in the letter, after another example of a literary scholar reading a text, this time by Cicero, only to obsess again over the words and references, Seneca claims that he does not want to turn into someone who spends his time "trying to track down archaic words, neologisms, peculiar metaphors, and figures of speech"; instead, he wants to "listen to the philosophers" so as to direct "attention to our goal, which is happiness" (108.35). The literary scholar, for Seneca, wishes to find the truth behind the words: their references, histories, and how they create distinct meanings in different combinations. But Seneca reads texts differently by asking himself how he can become better as a result of what he encounters. This reorientation strikes me as instructive for readers of *Much Ado*. If we view its characters not as literary scholars who scour the text for clues and interpretations, and instead as philosophers-in-training who wish to become better, we can re-frame the play as a spiritual exercise of self-care and divorce ourselves from a concern over truth and knowledge without dissolving into nihilism or postmodern affectation. Rather than interpret the play's rhythms of deception-revelation as epistemological in nature, we can detect a different current in the narrative, one in which characters turn away from the act of looking outward as a worthwhile activity. This latter mode is a more properly Stoic one, and it is one to which the play frequently turns. We might say that *Much Ado* twists Foucault's "why truth?" into "why representation?" and in doing so swerves away from the adoption of a critical framework that assumes a premium placed on knowledge. Why care in the first place if things we see stand for other things? In place of a concern for knowledge, *Much Ado* exercises a concern over care, over modes of self-inquiry that attempt to ensure the capacity to receive knowledge in the first place.

The play reflects an investment in this concern in its opening scenes, which tempt its audience to fit the dramatic action into a scheme of knowledge and revelation only to swerve into the more Stoic preoccupations of self-examination, capacity, and preparation. After seeing

Hero for the first time since his return from the war, Claudio appeals to Benedick for confirmation of his smitten reaction, first asking if Benedick "noted" her, and then if she is "not a modest young lady?" (1.1.154, 157). This latter question hangs in the air but is never quite answered. Instead, Benedick responds by considering the nature of the inquiry: "Do you question me as an honest man should do, for my simple true judgement? Or would you have me speak after my custom, as being a professed tyrant to their sex?" (1.1.158–61). The quality of the questioner preoccupies the questioned more than what was originally asked. Like Seneca or Epictetus, Benedick takes on the role of Stoic mentor consoling his pupil, but the consolation he offers demands first to know what priorities inform the inquiry. Even when pressed to answer sincerely, Benedick responds to a different query entirely as to whether he likes her: "Why, i'faith methinks she's too low for a high praise, too brown for a fair praise and too little for a great praise. Only this commendation I can afford her: that were she other than she is, she were unhandsome; and being no other but as she is, I do not like her" (1.1.163–67). His string of litotes performs a comic function by avoiding a direct description Hero, but the mechanics of this trope uncannily match those of Stoic indifference.

Benedick is far from a Stoic sage here. As blinkered as Claudio is in his lack of comprehension of Hero, Benedick has fallen prey to his own false judgments. These men, incapable of clear reflection, practice a form of Stoic care sutured onto a comic structure that in turn relies on the endless prismatic reflections of self-regard crowding out consideration of the ostensible object of discussion. Hero herself becomes lost in a sea of investigations of intention. Benedick responds again by asking if Claudio speaks "with a sad brow? Or do you play the flouting jack, to tell us Cupid is a good hare-finder and Vulcan a rare carpenter? Come, in what key shall a man take you to go in the song?" (1.1.172–76). Much as Benedick makes sure he knows what role he is to play in responding to Claudio, he wonders what role Claudio takes on in asking. This metatheatrical playfulness calls attention to the mechanics of the scene, but it also hints at the audience demanded by their behavior, a fun-house version of Epictetus' theatrical attentiveness. Claudio responds by not acknowledging Benedick's answer—which still isn't about the ostensible topic of discussion, Hero's modesty—and instead reports that "I can see yet without spectacles, and I see no such matter"; for Claudio, Hero is the "Sweetest lady that ever I looked on" (1.1.177–80).

Claudio now begins to mirror Benedick's concerns, rather than return to the question of Hero's worth. He claims he "would scarce trust myself, though I had sworn the contrary, if Hero would be my wife" (1.184–85). The formulation of the statement, that he would scarce trust himself, is idiomatic, but also belies the real theme of the dialogue thus far, buried under an apparent interest in whether Hero is modest: Is Claudio fit to judge whether Hero is modest in the first place? Even when confronted with the possibility that he loves Hero, Claudio admits that "If my passion change not shortly, God forbid it should be otherwise" (1.1.205–6). The evocation of "passion" here acts as a shorthand of affectation, but it may evoke the Stoic understanding of false judgment as well. By explicitly linking affectation to judgment, Claudio prioritizes the nature of his faculties of perception over the actual understanding of Hero's worth. Following his admission, more conditional "ifs" begin to pepper the exchange. Don Pedro, entering the scene, claims that "if you love her, for the lady is very well worthy" (1.1.207–8); later, he again proposes that "If thou dost love fair Hero, cherish it, / And I will break with her and with her father, / And thou shalt have her. Was't not to this end / that thou began'st to twist so fine a story?" (1.1.289–92). The persistent conditional tense reroutes focus onto the internal conditions that would give birth to action and delays judgment on the actions themselves.

Claudio's response once again turns (prophetically, as it turns out) on his own anxiety over the authenticity of words, rather than their content: "You speak this to fetch me in, my lord" (1.1.209). It is not until 60 lines after Claudio begins to question Benedick that any kind of conclusion arrives, and yet again the answer foregrounds the status of Hero within Claudio's consciousness, rather than an assessment of Hero herself: "That I love, her, I feel," Claudio reports, which sets up the assent of Don Pedro, who has entered the scene: "That she is worthy, I know" (1.1.214–15). Only Don Pedro explicitly links judgment to knowledge. Every other exchange zeroes in on the condition of the speaker or teases out a hypothetical situation that could emerge from the present moment. The dialogue sets up Benedick's fateful profession of romantic obstinacy, articulated in a confessional mode. He is so set in his opinion of women that "fire cannot melt out of me; I will die in it at the stake" (1.1.218). Even this affirmation of constancy protects a stance that is negatively defined: Benedick passionately believes that he does *not* know nor care to know the true nature of Hero's character. Don Pedro then offers the wager that springs the romantic plot into action: "I shall see thee, ere I die, look pale with love" (1.1.231).

The rapid rhythms of this scene clearly satirize the men's reliance on linguistic trickery at the expense of honesty, patriarchal ignorance of Hero's humanity, and solipsism in insisting on interrogating the topic at hand through their own experiences. These habits present rife opportunities for producing political and sociological implications. But the scene's status as comic should not prevent its potential to conduct philosophical work. Stoicism need not find itself in imitations of Seneca's drama. As Nussbaum elaborates, comedy and Stoicism in fact make natural, if strange, bedfellows:

> as a further weapon against excessive involvement with tragic characters, the Stoic uses humour and satire. The topic of Stoic hour sounds rather unpromising. But I believe it is not, and that one could do interesting research along those lines . . . the spectator is urged to find (his own or another's) excessive involvement in trivial things foolish, to laugh at the weepers. Such laughter cements the distance between hero and audience. ("Poetry and the Passions" 141)

Comedy can distance the reader from the text—or, in this scene, the player from the part. Benedick's repeated turn to question what roles he and Claudio play allows for a distancing-effect that encourages critical spectatorship for both the characters and the actual audience to the play. Benedick discourages attachment and instead allows for self-satire, a mode that encourages reflection on Claudio's motive and temperament.

There is a potential danger to this line of thinking. If we simply view the play as charting the course of a group of gentlemen who improve themselves through exploiting women, we expose Stoicism's deeply mis-ogynistic potential.[9] *Much Ado* counters this charge by exhibiting its most successful Stoic practices in Beatrice's self-cultivation. At the close of the celebrated scene of her overhearing the staged scene of her friends recount-ing (and perhaps creating) Benedick's amorous feelings for her, Beatrice seems less concerned with the veracity of what was said and more with her own responses:

> What fire is in mine ears? Can this be true?
> Stand I condemned for pride and scorn so much?
> Contempt, farewell; and maiden pride, adieu;
> No glory lives behind the back of such.
> And Benedick, love on, I will requite thee,
> Taming my wild heart to thy loving hand.
> If thou dost love, my kindness shall incite thee
> To bind our loves up in a holy band.
> For others say thou dost deserve, and I
> Believe it better than reportingly.

> (3.1.107–16)

Beatrice renders what could be a display of narcissism into a program for self-attentiveness. First examining her own responses, she begins with an appeal to knowledge: "Can this be true?" The speech then steers away from examining evidence for truth and instead prepares herself for truth's pos-sibility, marked with another persistent "if." Her prescribed regimen intends to rid herself of contempt and embrace kindness, and her decision to "requite" Benedick's love arrives through the clarification of her own opinion. The final paradoxical lines free the monologue from the charge of

---

[9] Foucault points out in *The Hermeneutics of the Subject* that *stultia*, the form of foolish restlessness that Seneca seeks to eliminate in his pupils, "has its moral version in the bearing of the *effeminatus*, of the man who is effeminate in the sense of being passive in relation to himself, unable to exercise *egkrateia*, mastery or sovereignty, over the self" (*Hermeneutics* 344). For treatments of gender in *Much Ado*, see Cook and Hays.

deception by claiming that her belief stems solely from within herself, that which is "better than" report. Her concern is not knowledge. Beatrice more closely embodies the ideal toward which Claudio and Benedick, in the earlier scene, stumble: an introspection that fine-tunes the ability to discern right from wrong brought about by alertness to and genuine feeling of embodied affects.

The two scenes surveyed thus far—the gentlemen discussing Claudio's intentions toward Hero, Beatrice's reflection on overhearing Benedick's feelings—allow the audience to withhold the temptation to find either a semblance of the truth through the scrim of incomplete knowledge (for the men, who is the real Hero? For Beatrice, do these people report accurately?) and instead discover a profoundly different set of questions that cannot help but sound, potentially, embarrassingly dated: How are these characters becoming better people? That is, how are they gaining access to virtue by questioning their inner selves? How can they realize their natures, their capacities? These lines of thought disengage us from any critical scrutiny on what is "really" happening and instead allow us to view the scenes as performances that train their pupils—the characters, the audience—to hone their capacity to parse out reason. The scenes realize a mode of practice in a theatrical form. The question, then, is not "Does Claudio properly know Hero?" or "Is Beatrice deceived?" but instead "Are these figures learning to realize fully their capacities by testing their ability to distinguish?" Crucially, the play poses this question in a distinctly *comedic* mien, one far removed from the bloody excesses of Senecan tragedy's cautionary lessons or the portentous political essays of early modern thinkers influenced by Stoicism, such as John Ford. Claudio, Benedick, and Don Pedro exhibit more interest in how the self can absorb reality and how they could evaluate what kind of person Hero actually is. Beatrice, too, realizes she must recast herself in a different mold and reorient her judgments to match inward reason. There is no interest in the sublime nothingness that Goddard locates in the play's fascination with human knowledge. Instead, illusion allows for reflection on how deceptions internally prevent the viewer from understanding the integrity of appearances at all. In this way the scenes twist away from Socratic molds as well. Rather than reduce forms to their origins, the discussants obsessively try to reduce their own perception to an exercise of reason. The scene thus bears a close resemblance to exactly the kind of consolation that Leonato mocks in his fury at offers to soothe his false mourning. But it does so in a comic key, rather than the tragic mode long focused on by scholarship of the era. It is through the familiar tropes of farce—self-centeredness, misguided romantic yearning, elaborate pranks—that Stoicism enacts its practice within the drama.

To analyze the play as simply a demonstration of classical philosophy does not properly do justice, however, to the particular early modern texture of Stoicism, which, on the surface, attempted to hammer Stoicism's "way of life" into just the kind of doctrinal set of concepts that the Stoics themselves critiqued. But the play evinces a path by which the vital practice of *askesis* survived in Shakespeare's day. The resonance between the relentlessly inward inquiries of Claudio, Benedick, and Beatrice and the techniques of self-attentiveness prescribed by the Stoics is not ahistorical or simply "theoretical" but the result of a historical circumstance by which the Stoic way of life slipped free of its reduction to a system of knowledge. In the next section, I will trace the genealogy by which *Much Ado* captures this inheritance in its celebrated practice of *wit*, a performative medium not dependent on knowledge and, I argue, a theatrical and staged realization of the philosophy's survival in performance.

3 A Certain Recklessness

One of the central ironies of Stoic *askesis*, which informs its early modern reception, is that while it was founded on practice, the telos of that practice could easily be misapprehended as a stultifying lack of activity. Early modern adaptations of classical works betray a sense of tentativeness in fully retaining the boldness of its defining focus on ways of life rather than doctrine. John Sanford, the translator of the 1567 English version of Epictetus' *Manual*, assures Queen Elizabeth in his dedicatory epistle that the original author, "although he were an Ethnicke, yet he were very godly & christian" (A4 v); shortly thereafter, in describing Epictetus' life, Sanford lays the groundwork for the stereotypical Stoic that would so preoccupy English drama and poetry:

> [H]e properly was a man, whose substance altogether did
> consiste in the reasonable mynde, accompting the mind only
> to be man, and ye body but an instrument ... he did so
> withdrawe himselfe from the care & love of outward things,
> so litle regarding hys body, or any thing there to belonging,
> that at *Rome* his house had no dore, for there was nothing at
> all but a beggarly bed of little value. (A7 v–r)

Both proto-Christian and overly cerebral, Epictetus exists for Sanford as
a prefiguration of proper religion and inactive misanthrope. Thomas James,
another English translator, prefaced his 1598 version of the *Manual*, retitled
The Moral Philosophie of the Stoicks, with an even more vituperative jab at
his source material: "The Stoicks are as odious unto some men, as they
themselves are hated of others: they call themselves professors hereof in
their gibing manner stockes, and not Stoickes, because of the affinitie of
their names" (A6 v). James, like Jonson, invents an "affinitie" both phonetic
and epistemological between the Stoics and "stocks," the contemporary
term of derision that signals senselessness and stupidity.

Similarly, Marcus Aurelius' sparse set of self-reminders in *Meditations*
becomes, in the early modern milieu, a much broader repository of received
wisdom massaged into a genre familiar to the era—the manual for a prince.
(Machiavelli's *The Prince* stands as the most famous example of this trend,
which also includes Erasmus' *Education of a Christian Prince* and King
James's *Basilikon Doron*.) As adapted—"translated" is too strict a term—
by Antonio de Guevara, the *Meditations* incorporates biographical sketches
of Marcus Aurelius alongside purported elements of his philosophy.[10]
Guevara still hopes to retain the hint of self-remedy with which Marcus
Aurelius imbued his work by titling his adaptation *Libro Aureo de Marco
Aurelio*, which in turn becomes "*The Golden Boke of Marcus Aurelius*" in
John Bourchier Berners's 1545 English translation. The performative quality of Marcus Aurelius' documentation of his own spiritual progress has
disappeared in this rendering. In place of the real-time acts of self-

---

[10] Guevara takes the biographical material from the spurious *Historia Augusta*,
which had enjoyed new popularity in Erasmus' 1518 edition. See Mezzatesta.

examination are shopworn sentiments sandwiched between hagiographic stories, as when Guevara describes Marcus Aurelius hearing news of insurrection in imperial territories. "The good emperour heringe these tidyngs," Guevara (through Berners) reports, "though he felte it inwardely as a man, yet he feyned it outwardly as a discrete man with a sadde countenance, and made fewe words." Marcus Aurelius then visits the territories and quells the possibility of war, and the episode closes with a pithy declaration that sticks a neat bow onto the anecdote: "Lyttel occasion suffiseth to them that be naturally of ill inclinations, to departe and sprede through countreys to do harme: therfore he sent them of his house to the intent, that by occasion of the warre, they shulde not leade an ill lyfe" (37–38). The tinge of actual Stoic principle colors the story, but Marcus Aurelius presents another unfeeling stock, absorbing his sadness and doling out Bowdlerized versions of his tenet that inward intent must precede action.

Seneca's Stoic works became similarly flattened into a medium that effectively robs it of its more vital dimensions. Instead of becoming a source of meditation for the reader that demands lived experience as complement to textual contemplation, works like Seneca's *Letters on Ethics* and *Natural Philosophy* found homes in advanced grammar lessons, to be copied by rote by students. Peter Mack, in an examination of Roger Ascham's popular pedagogical work *The Schoolmaster*, explains the process by which most students would encounter Seneca and other Latin authors:

> After the master and pupil have together construed the Latin text into English orally several times, the pupil must make his own written translation of the Latin. After checking the translation, the master should take away the Latin text and after about an hour ask the pupil to translate his own English version back into Latin. The pupil's version can then be compared with Cicero's original in order to bring out ways of improving the pupil's Latin. For Ascham the rules of concord are best taught and reinforced through examples. (31–32)

This dry dismemberment of the text realizes precisely the fate Seneca dreaded for Virgil in Letter 108, in which philosophical engagement becomes sacrificed for the production of knowledge. Fragments of Seneca weave through early English drama, perhaps as a result of his inclusion on humanist syllabi.[11] The apprehension of Seneca's writing as a philosophical whole in English remains elusive until Thomas Lodge's massive translation of his nondramatic texts in 1614. Even then, efforts to tame Seneca's work into more easily digested sets of ideas, rather than reproduce his works as performative prompts, persisted. In his preface Lodge addresses the beneficial effects of reading the fruits of his labors: "Would God Christians would endeavour to practice his good precepts, to reform their owne in seeing his errours; and perceiving so great of learning from a Pagan's pen, ayme at the true light of devotion and pietie, which becometh Christians. Learne him in these good lessons, and commit them to memory" (*Works* B5 v). Again we encounter the apologia of translating a pre-Christian author, coupled this time with a direct link to the grammar exercises that reduced Seneca to a repository of exercises and apothegms. Lodge's "good lessons" recalls the memorization of Seneca's "sentences," or *sententiae:* nuggets of wisdom that can be tucked away and recited at will.

Roughly 250 pages after Lodge makes this point, his directive is contradicted by Seneca himself. Letter 23 from *Letters on Ethics* (translated by Lodge as "The Epistles of Lucius Annaeus Seneca the Philosopher") mostly consists of a substantial critique of memorization and learning. Seneca notes, in Lodge's translation, that children are given "sentences" to memorize because

> a childish wit can comprehend them, being as yet uncapable
> of a more certaine and solid science. A complete man hath
> no honour to gather nose-gayes, to stay him selfe and build
> on certain usuall or few wordes, and to trust unto his
> memorie, hee ought to trust himselfe. Let him speake
> these but not retaine them: for it is a base thing for an olde
> man, or such a one as is stept in yeares to be wise in nothing

---

[11] For a treatment of Stoicism in early modern tragedy, see Braden.

> but his note-booke. This said *Zeno*, what sayest thou? This
> *Cleanthes*, but what thou? How long art thou directed by
> others? both command and say what shall be committed to
> memorie, and produce something of thine owne. (*Works*
> 221)

The authors Seneca selects as examples of rote, childish learning are telling. Both Zeno and Cleanthes are Greek Stoics, antecedents to the philosophy as developed by Seneca and other Romans. In warning against simply regurgitating the words of these thinkers, Seneca affords a reflection of his own project. His version of Stoicism cannot simply be simplified as a reiteration of classical precedent, and neither should the student of Stoicism treat philosophical texts as mere "nose-gayes" to be collected—even though Lodge encourages readers to do precisely that. The disdain on display here links to a sustained critique of learning that Seneca maintains throughout the *Letters*; most famous, perhaps is Letter 88, which begins with a blunt dismissal of liberal studies: "Thou desirest to know what I thinke concerning liberal studies. I admire none, I number none among those things to be good, whose end is for gaine. Hired workmanships they are, so farre profitable, as they prepare, and not determine the wit." (*Letters* 365). Justus Lipsius, the Flemish Neo-Stoic who provided brief prefaces to each of the letters in Lodge's edition, lightly amends Seneca's distaste in his opening gloss: "But although they doe not leade, yet they helpe: that is, they further and prepare" (*Letters* 365). *Pace* Lipsius, Seneca assuredly does not state, here, that the liberal arts "helpe" anything; his point is that focus on the liberal arts as their own end distracts from the pursuit of wisdom through philosophy. That his work, in the early modern era, would be used as an instrument of grammar thus provides a distinct irony.

In attempting to make Stoicism more doctrinal, systematic, and textual, early modern translations and adaptations suppressed the more theatrical elements of *askesis* that demand bodily engagement. They also reduced the philosophy to a repository of knowledge that must be learned, rather than the practice of dismissing knowledge as the criterion for advancement to the truth. Such an understanding is the kind exemplified by readings of *Much Ado* that evaluate its characters' trajectories as Ascham-esque educations through nuggets of wisdom, as if they must collect Senecan "nose-gayes" of accurate knowledge in order to better understand what truthfully is going on. But early modern translators' focus on knowledge does not mean Stoic preoccupations with philosophy as a way of life were wrung completely dry, however. Stoic embodiment survived the transition into more academic understandings of the philosophy partially through the translation of Cicero, a figure whose relationship to Stoicism is not as straightforward as that of Epictetus, Marcus Aurelius, or Seneca. Cicero's ambivalence toward Stoicism could perhaps find more purchase in early modern England, caught as it was in a fraught relationship with classical philosophers' simultaneous humanist appeal, as masters of rhetorical form, and Christian alienation, as pagan precursors. Cicero's work, fundamental as it is to the conduct books that helped define our understandings of early modern subjectivity and provide ample fodder for dramatic meditation, also gives us a genealogical connection to *Much Ado*—and thus provides a Trojan Horse for Stoic *askesis* to work its way into the play's cultural milieu. This connection is worth mapping out more thoroughly.

For Cicero, the Stoics had admirable philosophical aims: a valorization of wisdom, a belief in the interconnectedness of the universe. But they lacked the ability to convey this wisdom effectively. Cicero lays out the nature of his criticism in the introduction to *Stoic Paradoxes*. (This criticism would be familiar to some readers in the Renaissance because of its translation into English in 1569 by Thomas Newton, which I quote here.) In considering a figure thought to be one of the few genuine Stoic sages, Cicero concedes that as Cato was "a ryght and perfect Stoike," he "dooth both thincke those thinges which the vulgare people allowe not, and is also of that sect of Philosophers, which care not for elegancie of speache and floures of eloquence: neither dilate and amplifie their argumentes, but with breafe questions and Interrogatories (as it were withe certaine prickes or points) prosecute their reasons and dispatch their purposed intentes." In other words, even the most perfect Stoic did not find use for elegant speech, instead favoring the sparse, "hopping" style that William Fitzgerald claims was "characteristic of the Senecan manner" and often mimicked by Neo-Stoics like Lipsius (280). Cicero's preface continues: "But there is nothing so incredible, but the same by artificial handling may be made credible, ther is nothing so rude and barbarous, but by eloquence it may be polished, and scoured cleane. Consideringe and revolving these thinges in my mind, I adventured further then this Cato, of whom I speake" (*Booke* A2 v–r) This passage serves as a microcosm of Cicero's much larger project of connecting rhetoric to philosophy.[12] For Cicero, the Stoics had the right idea but lacked the proper eloquence, while conversely fantastic eloquence alone could never compensate for a lack of virtuous thought.

In *De Oratore*, composed approximately eight years earlier than *Stoic Paradoxes*, the Stoics similarly figure as a both admired and castigated school of thought that had potential but needed a clearer medium. That medium, for Cicero, is his title subject, oration. *De Oratore* takes the form of a dialogue, and in the second book, one of its main interlocutors, Antonius, surveys various philosophical schools of thought and weighs each by the Ciceronian standard of how they can synthesize communicability and wisdom. The Stoic, he proposes, is

> of no help whatsoever here, since he does not teach me to find what to say. In fact, he actually even hinders me, because he discovers many things that he says are absolutely insoluble, and the way of talking that he employs is neither clear, nor expansive and steadily flowing, but meager, dry, cramped, and disjoined. If anyone approves of this style, he will at least have to acknowledge that it is unsuitable for an orator. (*Oratore* 164–65)

Antonius' charge complements Cicero's praise of theatrical skill in the introduction to *De Oratore*. Cicero asks first "Surely I don't need to add anything about delivery?" before answering what seems to be a rhetorical question. Oration, he proclaims, "must be regulated by the movement of the body, by gesture, by facial expression, and by inflecting and varying the voice. Just how much effort this requires,

---

[12] It is one of the ironies of Cicero's legacy that he became reduced in part to grammatical example for schoolchildren, a status that stands in stark contrast to the philosopher's actual belief in the philosophical possibilities of oration.

even by itself, is indicated by the trivial art of actors on the stage. For although every one of them strives to regulate his facial expression, voice, and movement, we all know how really few actors there are, and have been, whom we can watch without irritation" (*Oratore* 61). The Stoics lack the ability to communicate properly while actors lack the ability to transcend the triviality of their sole mastery of delivery. The implication is that the Stoics provide the profundity that actors lack, and conversely, stage performers could lend to the Stoics the craft of delivery to realize better their philosophical potential.

In book three, Crassus, building on Antonius' principles and discussing how they might be implemented, allows that oratorical style is ultimately an exercise in unity. The terms of his description resonate with Stoic principles of universal interconnectivity and vibrant *pneuma*; Cicero's modern translators James M. May and Jakob Wisse note that the idea is of "Stoic origin" (*Oratore* 279 n.236). Crassus' explanation warrants quotation at length:

> [I]n the case of speech, nature itself has forged the same wondrous pattern as it has in the majority of other things: what possesses the greatest utility at the same time has the most dignity, and often even the most beauty. For the sake of the preservation and safety of all things, the natural disposition of our entire universe is such, as we can see, that the heavens are spherical; that the earth stands in the middle and maintains this position because of the tendency of its inherent force; that the sun travels around it, sinking until it reaches the winter constellation; and then rising gradually in the opposite direction; that the moon receives the light of the sun as it approaches and withdraws from it; and that the five planets complete the same orbit as sun and moon, but with different motions and courses. This order has such force, that even a slight modification would make its coherence impossible, and also such beauty that a more magnificent spectacle cannot even be imagined. (*Oratore* 278–79)

Crassus' rapturous ode to order expands its philosophical implications as it contracts its focus, from universe to heavens to earth, before considering the sun, moon, and other planets that orbit in tandem. Like Achilles' shield, the universe fractally reproduces balance in each of its iterations, from the miniature to the cosmic.[13] Unlike Homer's ekphrasis, Crassus' disquisition follows the modest modifier "in the case of speech." Speech, Crassus suggests, contains the same elemental principles of nature as does the universe. The ability to speak, the ability to have style, is a realization of a core Stoic principle. With their stunted speech, the Stoics alone cannot make manifest the very ideals in which they so devoutly and obsessively believe. They need, as Cicero has implied in *Stoic Paradoxes*, good communication skills as a complete manifestation of their ideals. Cicero, though Crassus, seizes a potential Stoic sympathy with performance that eludes its early modern dramatic avatars.

While this sympathy has been removed from overt early modern citations of Stoic works, it lingers more tacitly in one of the most influential pieces of performance theory in the era, Baldassare Castiglione's *The Book of the Courtier*. Castiglione's manual patterns itself on *De Oratore* in ways explicit and elusive. One of Castiglione's more coy references to Cicero's work occurs in perhaps its most famous section, a debate between Canossa, the primary speaker in book one, and a few of his interlocutors about whether grace is learned. The group has just settled on the topic of discussion that will preoccupy them for the rest of the text: enumerating the criteria of a "perfect Courtyer." (I quote here from Thomas Hoby's 1561 translation.) The question at hand is whether the perfect courtier could learn grace as he would other skills, such as archery or horsemanship. Canossa, whose disquisitions occupy much of the first book, answers that grace cannot emerge from simple emulation. He first relays a brief anecdote about a colleague who imitates a peculiar physical tic of the Prince of Aragon. "And manye such there are," Canossa continues, "that thynke they doe much, so they resemble a great man in somewhat, and take amny tymes the thynge in hym that woorst becommeth hym." But if grace cannot be emulated, it still can be practiced through the paradoxical concealment of the effort needed to attain it. One must, Canossa claims, "eschew as much as

---

[13] See *The Iliad* 18.551–600.

a man may, and as a sharp and daungerous rock, Affectation or curiosity and (to speak a new word) to use in every thing a certain Reckelesnes, to cover art withal." The "new word" here is the Italian *sprezzatura*, the famously untranslatable sense of aristocratic nonchalance that signals power while effacing any betrayal of power's exercise. Canossa nimbly escapes the trap set up by the premise of the question of learning grace—if one cannot, then one cannot learn to be a courtier; if one can, then grace becomes sullied by the whiff of labor—by claiming that the courtier learns "a very art that appeereth not to be art" (53).

The roots of *sprezzatura* can be found in Castiglione's source material. As much as it has become a metonymic quality of early modernity, *sprezzatura* does not so much amend its classical source as it does move one of *De Oratore*'s topics from the margins to the center. What is grace for Castiglione was, for Cicero, an example of wit. *Dissimulatio*, translated often as "dissembling," arrives in book two of *De Oratore* as a possible technique of persuasion through gentle jesting. After appeals from his conversation partners, Caesar, an orator renowned for his cleverness, begins anatomizing various forms of rhetorical humor that could be used to win over an audience. He first identifies irony as "saying something different from what you think" before noting that "Socrates by his refined wit far excelled all others in this 'irony,' this dissembling," by "combining wit with seriousness" (*Oratore*, 198–99). He then gives examples of *dissimulatio*, a related kind of maneuver, albeit one that is "a bit trivial" and more "suitable for actors in mimes" than the orator (200). He follows with an example of this cousin to irony, a story that involves one Nasica, who was told by his friend Ennius' maid that her master was not home, even though Nasica knew he was. Later, when Ennius came to visit, Nasica answered the door and informed him that he himself was not home. The punchline depends on the obviousness of Nasica's lie contrasted with his apparent naiveté: "Nasica replied, 'You're shameless! I believed your maid when I asked you and she said you were not home—and you do not believe me when I tell you the same thing personally?'" (200). Nasica's feigned lack of knowledge works as humor, but its construction, which depends on signaling a lack of understanding as a demonstration of power, anticipates Castiglione's valorization of an "art that conceals itself." Furthermore, the context of the section of *De Oratore* that Castiglione amends in his discussion of grace becomes hidden in a metatextual exercise of the very *sprezzatura* that Canossa describes. As Rebecca Helfer notes, Castiglione offers a proper homage to Cicero by denying any outright trace of homage at all: "Canossa at once conceals and reveals the main speakers of Cicero's *On the Orator*, Crassus and Antonius, as masters of such dissimulation" (336). The art of concealment extends to the occlusion of borrowing from source material.

It is this focus on wit, and wit's willful rejection of knowledge, that allows Castiglione's appropriation of Cicero to serve as a primal scene, of sorts, of *Much Ado*'s persistent exercises of performed indifference. Wit-as-dissimulation appears in *De Oratore* in other exemplary cases and even, as Jennifer Richards has illuminated, occupies a central role in the work's structure. Richards notes that Antonius' "promise to share his 'personal views' is no straightforward recantation; rather, it is an example of a 'jest' included in Julius's list of witticisms under the name of dissimulation (pretending not to understand what you understand perfectly)" (470) In other words, Cicero practices a fundamental form of *dissimulatio* by repeatedly couching his speakers' ideas in self-effacing asides, thus concealing the actual importance of deception in oratory. Helfer detects in this playfulness a form of theatricality. "Antonius," she notes, "thus uses wit to reveal what he usually conceals, the performance at play in oratory, and in the process unmasks his own performative persona" (339). Cicero offers playful hints as to how wit informs the structure in *De Oratore* in his introduction of Crassus and Antonius, in the prologue to book two, where Cicero notes the two speakers' lack of education. Crassus' "contact with learning had not extended beyond the opportunities afforded him by the elementary education normal for a boy" whereas Antonius "was entirely unacquainted with any instruction whatsoever." As a result, their reputations gained fearsomeness through the implication that they could surpass the skills of those who actively attempted to learn their skills:

> For if men without a theoretical background had attained
> a   consummate   degree   of   practical   insight   and   an

unbelievable level of eloquence, all of our labor, they imagined, would appear worthless, and the devotion that our
excellent and intelligent father gave to seeing us educated
would seem mere folly. (*Oratore* 125)

The two primary interlocutors in *De Oratore*, then, couch their virtu-
osity in the kind of recklessness that Castiglione will later feature as the
defining quality of the courtier. As an example of this idea's currency,
Philip Sidney, in his "Defence of Poesy," seizes on deception as the
primary characteristic of the two orators. Sidney, though, leaves no
doubt as to whether their lack of learning itself comprised a performed
skill, noting that Antonius "pretended not to know art" and Crassus
"not to set by it, because with a plain sensibleness they might win
credit of popular ears" (247).

Another subtle, though less noticed, link to Castiglione's source material
is his acknowledgement of Stoicism as *sprezzatura*'s ambivalent patron. In
book two, a new interlocutor, Frederick, takes center stage to begin crafting
the means by which the ideals Canossa sketched out in book one can be
realized in practice. This section acts as a rough analogue to Crassus' efforts
in *De Oratore* to implement a stylistic execution of Antonius' outline of
oration's goals. Frederick evokes the Stoics in a similar fashion to Crassus,
as well. For both, Stoicism offers ideal versions of harmony by which the
subject at hand—oration, courtiership—can be inspired. It "behoverth oure
Courtier," Frederick notes, to

> order the tenour of his life after suche a trade, that the whole
> may be answerable unto these partes, and see the selfe same
> to bee always and in every thing suche, that it disagree not
> from it selfe, but make one body of all these good qualities,
> so that everye deede of his may be compact and framed of al
> the vertues, as the Stoikes say the duetie of a wiseman is:
> although not withstanding alwaies one virtue is the princi-
> pall, but all are so knit and linked one to an other, that they
> tende to one ende, and all may bee applied and serve to
> every purpose. (107–8)

Here, the vision of universally expanding harmony imagined as the model of proper speech by Crassus becomes, in an early modern context, both explicitly named as Stoic and relocated from oration back into its original context of "virtue." The principal virtue, unnamed but undoubtedly that of reason, is that to which all other qualities are tethered. Frederick develops this vision further by emphasizing how a unity of virtue becomes assembled through the "comparison and (as it were) contrariety of the one": that is, the perfect courtier must, like Gonzalo's commonwealth in *The Tempest*, balance opposites in order to reach equilibrium.[14] At stake here, though —and this perhaps is the early modern twist, and the clear thematic kinship to *Much Ado*—is not something as lofty as the Stoic goal of harmony with nature as it is the execution of social power. The section that begins with an excursus on Stoicism ends with a conclusion that re-grounds the discussion in the practicalities of the courtier's art. Frederick finishes by deducing that, "little speaking muche doing, and not praising a mannes owne selfe in commendable deedes, dissemblyng them after an honeste sorte, dooeth increase both the one vertue and the other in a person that can discreatly use this trade" (108). Stoicism's preoccupation with cosmic order becomes converted into a recommendation that ironically echoes the characteristic of Stoicism that Cicero critiqued, its lack of oration. Here, though, "little speaking" becomes instrumentalized as the means by which the courtier can better "discreately use this trade"—how, in other words, the courtier can once again cover the tracks of its labor, here not as a fanciful meditation on grace but instead as a valuable aspect of a craft.

This treatment of Stoicism exemplifies a broader pattern in *The Courtier* of rendering ineffable qualities of the courtier such as grace, humor, and even the concealment of learning itself into teachable skills. Thomas Hoby, in his introduction to his English translation, emphasizes that, like Stoic *askesis*, this learning is resolutely bodily. He connects his textual translation

---

[14] Gonzalo reports to the sneering Sebastian that "I'th' commonwealth I would by contraries / Execture all things, for no kind of traffic / Would I admit; no name of magistrate; / Letters should not be known; riches, poverty / And use of service, none" (2.1.148–53). The lines borrow from Florio's translation of Montaigne's "Of the Caniballes."

to the corporeal translation taken on by the book's potential acolyte. In defending his project, Hoby notes that translating the classics "doeth not only not hinder learning, but it furthereth it, yea it is learning it self"; in other words, translating both gives access to wisdom and creates wisdom in its undertaking. Hoby provides a litany of salutary effects of studying works in other languages before concluding that it creates "a gap for others to folow their steppes, and a vertuous exercise for the unlatined to come by learning, and to fill their minde with the morall vertues, and their body with civyll condicions, that they maye bothe talke freely in all company, live uprightly though there were no lawes, and be in a readinesse against all kinde of worldlye chaunces that happen" (7). The pursuit of wisdom through the study of ancient texts, in particular the texts Hoby has linked explicitly to Castiglione, who "hath followed Cicero" (5), fills not only the mind with virtue but the body with "civyll condicions." The effect of studying a transmuted version of Ciceronian rhetoric, alchemized with the individual desires and pragmatic realities of the early modern court, is not only moral but performative.

This synthesis brings us back to my central argument in this section: that an aspect of Stoicism as practice survived, tacitly, in the early modern era—appropriately enough, in a disguise of sorts, garbed in the cloth of wit. Stoicism operates as an example of the performativity demanded by Castiglione's appropriation of Cicero. It exists in *The Courtier* as an ideal of witty self-concealment, effaced in its own concealment via *dissimulatio*. In its near-disappearance it models both the ideal, in terms of unity, and negative example, in terms of execution, of rhetoric. The Stoics lacked the ability to let speech gain the same cosmic balance with which they imbued the world. And yet the proper technique for achieving the Stoic's goals is *not* rhetorical excess. Instead, the aspiring student learns a mode of being that, for Castiglione at least, is resolutely corporeal. Though this kind of Stoic theatricality is relegated to the margins of *The Courtier* and *De Oratore*, its textual minimization does not attenuate its influence. Instead, for texts so obsessively circuitous and evasive in mapping their own heritage, Stoicism's occlusion becomes an ironic mark of its importance. We find here a way that Stoicism survived in the early modern era closer to the bodily, experiential way of life that more straightforward scholarly modifications of Stoicism attempted to scrub clean in translations of the primary texts. To act as a Stoic was to veer away from knowledge, from even caring about truth, and instead to conceal its importance. In particular, *wit* affords the student of Cicero or Castiglione the means of this mode of performance that avoids pomposity on the one hand and misanthropic stupor on the other. Wit allows a disposition suited for civil conditions, a realization of *sprezzatura* that bestows grace, sans any trace of labor, onto its successful practitioner. Wit is notably performative: it is oratorical, spectacular, and in a sense staged. And wit is, in the words of Ian Munro, "the common currency" of *Much Ado*, the "means by which social and cultural relationships in the play are negotiated" (90). As such, if we see wit as one of the ways Stoicism survived as performance and escaped the clutches of its deadening and anti-Stoic attenuation in direct translation, I would suggest that *Much Ado About Nothing* stages occasions of Stoic practice within its theatrical and comic structure. It does so through its direct and well-documented engagement with Castiglione—as Philip Collington observes, "Castiglione is 'everywhere' in *Much Ado*, an intellectual presence to which Shakespeare responds"(284)—but it also acts as its own kind of exercise where we join Claudio, Benedick, and Beatrice as pupils, unwilling or not, who learn to look away from knowledge and fine-tune our sense of attentiveness.[15] The play does not reproduce Stoic sentiments; it behaves in a Stoic manner.

4 No More Than Reason

Much Ado About Nothing foregrounds one usage of wit in its use of proverbs and epigrams, those nuggets of wisdom so disliked by Leonato, to stand in for the seemingly more vital knowledge gained from experience. The play's disdain for this shallow genre of wit, however, acts as its own dramaturgical *dissimulatio* by distracting from the subtle methods by which the play proffers a more profound strain of wit as a Stoic performance of indifference. Witness, for instance, the way that Beatrice uses, not simply reproduces, epigrammatic speech in her reply to her uncle lightly urging her towards

---

[15] See Collington and Scott.

marriage. "You may light upon a husband that hath no beard," suggests Leonato, to which Beatrice replies:

> What should I do with him? Dress him in my apparel and make him my waiting-gentlewoman? He that hath a beard is more than a youth, and he that hath no beard is less than a man; and he that is more than a youth is not for me, and he that is less than a man, I am not for him. Therefore I will even take sixpence in earnest of the bearward and lead his apes into hell. (2.1.28–35)

The speech begins with Beatrice, who has just mocked beards as uncomfortable and scratchy, swiftly switching positions to reference the common belief that a lack of facial hair connotes effeminacy. She then expounds on her conundrum by offering a jesting proof, possibly a satire of the Aristotelian belief in virtue as a mean between extremes, before aurally linking "beard" to "bearward," one who takes care of bears, and connecting this image of animal husbandry to the contemporary belief that spinsters lead apes into hell, presumably because they lacked children to lead them to heaven. Leonato takes the bear-bait, asking "Well then, go you into hell?" and Beatrice answers with another sequence of imbricated references:

> No, but to the gate, and there will the devil meet me like an old cuckold with horns on his head, and say, "get you to heaven, Beatrice, get you to heaven. Here's no place for you maids!" So deliver I up my apes and away to Saint Peter fore the heavens. He shows me where the bachelors sit, and there live we as merry as the day is long. (2.1.37–43)

A pattern becomes discernable in this stream of imagery. The sonic or semantic logic of one phrase links partially to another, which in turn offers a connection to another agreed-upon convention, which in turn becomes an exemplary sinew to entangle a new idiom, and so on. In this case, the devil appears at the gates of the hell into which the spinsters lead apes and, in an aside offered purely for the spontaneous discovery of imagistic overlap,

Beatrice notes that the devil's horns echo the cuckold's horns. She then proceeds to heaven, which recognizes her maidenhead as virtuous and sits her next to bachelors. Having mocked beardless men as effeminate, she now anoints herself as masculine to possess the freedoms afforded to bachelors, the very kind she will later lament not having, in a moment of vengeful anger against Claudio: "O God, that I were a man! I would eat his heart in the marketplace" (4.1.304–305).

In these early scenes, Beatrice's intentions are more generous. She means in part to confuse and ultimately deter her uncle from questioning her lack of a husband. The employment of wit, here, steers away from the pursuit of knowledge. She also demonstrates a kind of intelligence missing from other, more shallow, epigram-wielding wits. Rather than attempt to "patch grief with proverbs," she patches the proverbs themselves by building a veritable world with its own internal logic, as such demonstrating a distinctly early modern use of wit that carries forth the classical Stoic goal of learning: to mobilize and cohere sayings into something new, rather than to collect them as individual signifiers of status. Recall Seneca's imperative in Letter 88: "both command and say what shall be committed to memorie, and produce something of thine owne." This mission of creative originality, not Lipsius' exhortation to memorize sentences for their own sake as vessels of learning, finds in Beatrice's speech an ideal vehicle. The use of idioms, not simply their citation but their instrumentality, recalls as well Foucault's lectures on Marcus Aurelius' *Meditations*. The "effect expected" from reading Marcus Aurelius' text, Foucault suggests, is "not to have understood what an author meant, but the creation of an equipment of true propositions for yourself, which really is your own"; furthermore, this process "is not a matter of putting together a hodgepodge of propositions from different places, but of building a solid framework of propositions that are valid as prescriptions, of true discourses that are at the same time principles of behavior" (*Hermeneutics* 358). The repurposing of what is read into an active, world-making way of life is thus "a kind of habit for the body" (*Hermeneutics* 359). Adopting the language of performance studies, we might say that Beatrice translates from the archive into the repertoire:

from the static textuality of recitation to the organic vitality of experience.[16]

The play opens with a comparison between these two paradigms of learning. When the messenger arrives to tell Leonato that Claudio has performed bravely in the war, and that Claudio's uncle (never mentioned again in the play) has felt so much joy "that joy could not show itself modest enough without a badge of bitterness," Leonato responds with a chiasmic platitude: "How much better it is to weep at joy than to joy at weeping!" (1.1.21–22, 26–27). The two exchange idioms without any of the playful mutability exhibited by Beatrice, a contrast made clearer moments later, when she questions the messenger using a nickname for Benedick. "I pray you," she asks, "is Signor Mountanto returned from the wars or no?" (1.1.28–29). The more literal-minded messenger does not follow, responding that he knows "none of that name." After being corrected, the messenger replies that Benedick has returned, which prompts Beatrice to weave another complex account out of aphorism and resonance:

> He set up bills here in Messina and challenged Cupid at the
> flight and my uncle's fool, reading the challenge, subscribed
> for Cupid and challenged him at the bird-bolt. I pray you,
> how many hath he killed and eaten in these wars? But how
> many hath he killed? For indeed I promised to eat all of his
> killing. (1.1.36–43)

The raw materials for this complex description consist of a set of commonplaces: handbills announce archery contests, archery contests require longer arrows, Cupid fires bird-bolts, fools subvert the rules, and so on; the charge to eat all of Benedick's "killing" mocks him for his inefficacy as a warrior and thus overlays his military skills onto his amorous abilities. The messenger, moments before comfortably lobbing adages as a means of approximating proper emotional conduct, remains confused: "He hath done good service, lady, in these wars" (1.1.45–46). Unable to use his sayings as equipment, he concerns himself only with how expressions reflect

[16] I borrow the paradigmatic distinction of archive and repertoire from Taylor.

knowledge, and thus may help us discover the truth, while Beatrice floridly demonstrates her witty indifference to even the question of Benedick's service and instead sharpens her own ability to evince a "principle of behavior," a way of cultivating a proper disposition toward the world rather than validating the authenticity of what inhabits it.

The play also tests our own capacity, as audience members and readers, to rely on knowledge as the proper criterion for experiencing the drama. *Much Ado* tempts us into thinking its plot depends upon access to knowledge, but continually prioritizes the cultivation of dispositions over the revelation of facts. It presses us to make ethical valuations based on how characters respond to representations rather than how they interrogate them as a medium of learning the truth. One such technique by which it challenges our expectations is to play with the convention of bystanders gaining access, intentionally or not, to privileged knowledge that it would benefit someone else to hear. The major hinge on which the main plot hangs, the revelation of Don John's scheme to fool Claudio into believing that Hero has been unfaithful, seems to relate necessary information. However, before this revelation takes place, the audience has been trained to cultivate its own critical indifference to epistemological inquiry. One of the first instances of the overhearing convention takes place when we learn, in the second scene, that an earlier exchange between Claudio and Don Pedro had been misapprehended by "a man" of Antonio's. Leonato's brother relates to him that "the prince discovered to Claudio that he loved my niece your daughter, and meant to acknowledge it this night in a dance, and if he found her accordant, he meant to take the present time by the top and instantly break with you of it" (1.2.19–14). We know that, despite Antonio's insistence that his spy is a "good sharp fellow," he has mistakenly heard only some of Don Pedro's plan to "tell fair Hero I am Claudio; / and in her bosom I'll unclasp my heart / And take her hearing prisoner with the force / And strong encounter of my amorous tale" (1.1.303–06). Presumably he has only heard the description of what he will do as Claudio, not that he will then break the news to Leonato that Claudio in fact loves Hero, not him. Leonato's response is not to question the sharp fellow but instead to "hold it as a dream till it appear itself," to hold the mental image as true without investigating its correspondence with reason.

This is the first layer of misunderstanding, onto which is mapped another revelation that, along with Antonio's servant, Borachio had similarly overheard Don Pedro's plan. "I whipped me behind the arras," Borachio excitedly reports to Don John in a parallel scene, "and there heard it agreed upon that the prince should woo Hero for himself, and having obtained her, give her to Count Claudio" (1.3.56–59). Borachio's news leads to Don John swiftly misleading Claudio into thinking that Don Pedro *actually is* wooing Hero, which Claudio believes. But no actual secrets exist in Claudio's gulling. There is no plot to deceive anyone except, perhaps, the hapless Hero, who is supposed to believe that Don Pedro is Claudio before Claudio himself appears. Claudio's misunderstanding arises not because of withheld knowledge but because of improper attitudes toward the importance of truth. Borachio's deception hinges on telling Claudio *what he already knows*. Don Pedro has already claimed, to Claudio, that he will unclasp his heart and "take her hearing prisoner." What Don John tells Claudio, later, is that Don Pedro "is enamoured on Hero," which he knows because he "heard him swear his affection"; Borachio confirms that Don Pedro "swore he would marry her tonight" (2.1.149, 153–4). No change of knowledge actually occurs; no play on "nothing" can signify the gaps among what is noted, known, or truthful. What differs in Claudio from his initial conference with Don Pedro to his later discussion with Don John is his capacity to judge, his ability to evaluate how knowledge may have the appearance of truth or not. Claudio must assume that Don John's version of the same story given to him by Don Pedro is more worthy to be deemed accurate. The many aesthetic misdirections at play—Claudio dresses as Benedick; Leonato mishears one account of what occurred; Don John promises to woo as Claudio; and so on—practice a kind of *sprezzatura* on the audience by disguising the rigor of what is essentially an exercise of our judgment alongside a test of Claudio, which he fails. These early scenes hint that we will witness a straightforward revelation of knowledge, an Aristotelian *peripeteia* by which the unknown becomes known, but such a climax never arrives. Instead, they wittily swerve away from the elevation of knowledge as requirement for suspense.

It is telling that shortly after hearing Claudio morosely confess his unhappiness at Don Pedro claiming Hero, Benedick laments hearing Beatrice call him a fool by expressing anger at her "disposition": "It may be I go under that title because I am merry. Yea, but so I am apt to do myself wrong. I am not so reputed; it is the base, though bitter, disposition of Beatrice that puts the world into her person and so gives me out. Well, I'll be revenged as I may" (2.1.187–91). Benedick focuses less on the truth behind what Beatrice says and more on how Beatrice positions herself relative to the world. And Claudio himself, before the non-deception exercised by Don John, frames his love for Hero as an inward-looking evaluation of his passions, in the Stoic sense of judgment rather than as any objective change in Hero herself: "But now I am returned, and that war-thoughts / Have left their places vacant, in their rooms / Come thronging soft and delicate desires, / All prompting me how fair young Hero is, / Saying I liked her ere I went to wars" (1.1.282–86). The characterological shift from war-hero to lover depends on Claudio processing and inwardly curating the placement of desire, personified here as a tenant in his cognitive faculties. Claudio is not particularly witty; the Stoic performance of humor demonstrated by Beatrice finds no echo in his use of language. But the play demonstrates its own narrative wit in the comic effortlessness with which it distracts its audience and readers from the importance of approaching the truth through knowledge. This pattern becomes perfectly emblematized in the moment of Hero's own "revelation" to Claudio, which is withheld from the audience by that simplest of theatrical concealments, the whisper: "My cousin tells him in his ear that he is in her heart," reports Beatrice (2.1.289–90). It is not difficult to know what she says—it is impossible. The audience does not become surrogate detectives, as in a modern novel, sifting for clues.[17] Instead we become critical spectators examining our own processes of judgement. In the early modern milieu of the comedy of

---

[17] This metaphor, which ties together the reader's experience with the sleuthing figure at the core of many modern novels, originates with Miller, who is in turn influenced by the later Foucault of *Discipline and Punish*.

manners, the Stoic philosophical attitude, so scorned by Leonato, appears as a viable mode of dramaturgy for the play in which he resides.

The observation I am making here, that *Much Ado About Nothing* appears to place a premium on the acquisition of knowledge but in fact practices a deft maneuvering around the placement of knowledge as essential for its plot to function, echoes a careful reading of the play by Derek Gottlieb, who similarly notes that Claudio, in the speech that declares his feelings for Hero, demonstrates an "attitudinal comportment toward Hero as toward one beloved" that "precedes any recognition of her 'fairness' as a predicate.' Nowhere in this scene is there any mention of Hero's virtue or honor" (65). Gottlieb's analysis follows the influential philosophical tradition practiced by Stanley Cavell, whose substantial body of work defies easy disciplinary categorization. Suffice it to say that in *Disowning Knowledge*, a collection of essays on Shakespeare, he identifies a skeptical position in which characters demand appeals to verification that cannot be substantiated. These figures run aground on the shores of their own simultaneous dependence on language and realization of language's lack of ability to correspond to a universally shared set of meanings. (Cavell's readings follow his engagement with the later work of Ludwig Wittgenstein.) Cavell's skeptics exist in an overwhelming sea of doubt, unsure of the stability of knowledge yet in denial of language's capacity to express. Gottlieb extends Cavell's observations from the Shakespearean tragedies and romance covered in *Disowning Knowledge* to comedies like *Much Ado*, and in this way, Gottlieb owes more to Cavell's work on film, the specifically Hollywood "comedies of remarriage" surveyed in Cavell's *Pursuits of Happiness*. (*Much Ado* may not be as out of place in this canon as its historical difference first suggests; Marjorie Garber observes that the play is a forerunner to "the bantering, witty, sophisticated romantic plots that emerges in the films of the 1930s and 1940s" (371), and explicitly connects this similarity to Cavell's work.) In *Pursuits*, Cavell connects the pattern of remarriage displayed in these to the means by which Wittgenstein suggests we become lured by the assurance of knowledge only to find that we are bound to language and that language denies any universal set of correspondences with the world. As Cavell puts it:

> The temptation to metaphysics becomes in Wittgenstein a will to emptiness, to thoughtless thought; and this is something that has to be resisted again and again, because the temptation to speculation, however empty, is as natural to the human creature and its criticism is. Second, the idea that what happens to the philosophic mind when it attempts speculation beyond its means is that it transgresses something we want to call limits, is an idea that cannot as it stands constitute a serious term of criticism for Wittgenstein but must remain merely a 'picture,' however significant. (*Pursuits* 78)

The picture referenced here is an image that pretends to offer correspondence to the truth but can only lead to emptiness. For Cavell, the stakes here are nearly biblical: we are tempted out of the Eden of language into a doomed belief that we can know more than our language promises us at any given moment.

Much Ado, as Gottlieb notes, certainly tempts us with the lure of meaning, but my belief that the play practices a Stoic exercise on the audience differs in that, while Stoicism may not believe the philosopher could or should attempt to understand a larger order of knowledge that structures the world, they surely believe that such a higher divinity exists. As much as Stoic *askesis* trains the participant to disregard knowledge and focus instead on her inner faculties of reason, it does not preclude the possibility of truth existing—in fact, if anything, it simply venerates truth more, as it demands only the purified consciousness of sagacity in order to approach the capacity to discern the truth. Only sages can truly say that they can perceive the truth, that their assent to judgment coincides with an absolute order of the universe. And, as discussed earlier, Stoic sages were nearly an extinct species. We are all instead caught in the jaws of nearly infinite training, always maximizing our capacities rather than presuming to perceive with accuracy. Furthermore, Stoicism is normative; its most careful readers have rejected possible mutuality between Stoic practice and nihilism. Nussbaum directly critiques the ordinary language philosophy of Cavell in making this point. Stoicism's emphasis on philosophy as practical and practiced, not just intellectual, echoes Cavell because it "insists on a critical scrutiny of ordinary belief," but differs because it "gives a place to expert judgment that is absent from simpler versions, at least, of the ordinary belief view. When a doctor examines a patient, she will to some extent trust what the patient says about her condition. But she will also look and see with her own experiences and expertly trained eye" (*Therapy* 25).[18] In other words, the philosopher is not adrift in a sea of unknowability: she possesses experience and training that grants expertise. Stoicism relies on standardization in ways ordinary language philosophy does not.

I have embarked on this digression on how ordinary language philosophy fails to apprehend Stoicism to illuminate larger points about Stoic practice that help us better read *Much Ado* as the realization of Stoicism's performative capacities. Stoic performance sails between the Scylla of Platonic belief in forms and the Charybdis of Christian self-erasure, but it also resists negativism. The effect of *Much Ado*'s dramaturgy, which diverts pursuits of knowledge through its deployment of wit and deliberate plot confusion, is not an agon over the terror of meaninglessness. It is instead, to recall Foucault's salient question, to wonder why truth matters at all. Why should truth determine certainty? In this sense, a Stoic practice is closer to what James Kuzner labels "epistemological humility," the ability to be uncertain and in that uncertainty allow for political community (8). But I believe Stoicism is getting at something even stranger to our sensibilities: the notion that we cannot exist in humility of our knowledge if we never cared about knowledge in the first place. And yet, as Hadot and Nussbaum remind us, indifference does not connote a lack of concern over virtue. Indeed, the practice of performative indifference in the play seizes on a particular virtue, reason, that makes no appeal to knowledge and comprises the one principle we can actually control. The version of Stoicism that

---

[18] It is simplistic to conflate, as Nussbaum does here, nihilism with ordinary language philosophy. To believe that the meaning of language is coextensive with its use is also to believe in the possibility of also forging a fragile and vital sense of community, one untethered to an atomist relation of text to meaning. For a clear-eyed defense of ordinary language philosophy, see Moi; for an elaboration of its applicability to Shakespeare, see Beckwith, esp. 127–46.

survives through its adaptation in *The Courtier*, inherited by way of Cicero, still retains this focus even if—especially if—it professes a *sprezzatura* of nonchalance toward the truth.

And so I take seriously a conversation in *Much Ado* usually played for laughs: the exchange of assurances practiced by Beatrice and Benedick at the conclusion of the play that asserts reason as the impetus for their mutual affection. "Do you not love me?" asks Benedick. Beatrice responds: "Why, no, no more than reason"; she asks the same question of him, to which he replies "Troth no, no more than reason" (5.4.73, 77). Benedick's reflection upon his engagement lingers less on any evaluation of Beatrice. Instead, he thinks of love as a matter of discernment, of separating judgments: "In brief, since I do purpose to marry, I will think nothing to any purpose that the world can say against it; and therefore never flout at me for what I have said against it" (5.4.103–6). Beatrice and Benedick's vows to follow reason promises that they will engage with the present in acts of mutual predisposition. They make no appeals to knowledge of their affection, instead identifying the potential of communality in the application of discernment to the moment. In doing so they recall the lines of Marcus Aurelius, written as one of his daily reminders:

> Everywhere and at all times, it is up to you to rejoice piously at what is occurring *at the present moment*, to conduct yourself with justice towards the people who are *present here and now*, and to apply rules of discernment to your *present* presentations, so that nothing slips in that is not objective. (qtd. in Hadot, *Philosophy* 84)

Theirs is not a love of austere self-discipline, as my citation of the passage of Marcus Aurelius might suggest. It celebrates their bond in a distinctly early modern fashion, through their mutual use of wit, an ability to separate critically from texts, to synthesize material beyond their fragmentations, to defer knowledge and thus to realize comically Stoicism's goals. But the fundamental meaning of Marcus Aurelius' instruction doubles as a sort of marriage vow for the two lovers. Although the knowledge that they love one another has been fabricated by conspiring friends, each of their *comportments*, their attitudes to the present, has echoed the other's through the play. Like Beatrice, Benedick continuously engages with wit as the deconstruction and reconstruction of idiom, as critical playfulness that demonstrates Senecan learning. In the first scene of the play, confronted with Don Pedro's straightforward recitation of an old saying—"In time the savage bull doth bear the yoke"—Benedick responds by narrating an expansive picture: "the savage bull may, but if ever the sensible Benedick bear it, pluck off the bull's horns and set them in my forehead; and let me be vilely painted, and in such great letters as they write 'Here is good horse to hire', let them signify under my sign, 'Here you may see Benedick, the married man'" (1.1.244–49). The audience has been primed to see their commitment to reason as linked to their wit, and their wit to their judgment. Their assurances inhere to what is good rather than care about what is true.

If we follow this line of thinking, we release the play from the many interpretations of their engagement that ironize their affection. In the preface to the Norton edition of the play, Stephen Greenblatt finds its central depiction of courtship an ideal plaintiff for New Historicism: "Beatrice and Benedict constantly tantalize us with the possibility of an identity quite different from that of Claudio and Hero, an identity deliberately fashioned to resist the constant pressure of society. But that pressure finally prevails. Marriage is a social conspiracy" (342–43). Greenblatt's view is challenged in a footnote in the third Arden edition that appends Don Pedro's declaration to "fashion" the love between Beatrice and Benedick. Claire McEachern, the Arden editor, notes that for "some heartless critics," such as Greenblatt, "this language of artifice is proof that the ultimate union of Beatrice and Benedick is more indebted to social convention and machination than voluntary feeling" (2.1.340 n). But the Stoic would ask: why do we care so much about what is real or what is fashioned? Greenblatt and other New Historicists are deeply inspired by the work of Foucault, who is in turn deeply influenced by the Stoics, but their analysis relies on Foucault's ultimate endpoint of the care of the self—technologies of power—rather than dwelling on the narrower (but no less complex) understanding of "fashioning" that takes place in the Stoic texts that help pave the way for, but are ultimately independent of, the processes of objectivation taken up by

Christianity and modernity. The Stoics train their eyes on how the self relates to the self without recourse to wondering whether either self is authentic. The question at hand would instead be how Beatrice and Benedick relate to their own response to the courtship, not the courtship itself.

Their responses stand in stark contrast to the misuse of reason, figured as a *lack* of proper indifference to knowledge, as exercised by Claudio and Leonato, whose entangled misjudgments in the first two acts later become compounded into near-tragedy in the failed wedding between Claudio and Hero. We could view the events of this scene as a result of deception, and thus of incorrect knowledge, and of course this is partly true: Claudio has been "deceived" insofar as a false scene has apparently stood in for a real one as he believes he has seen Hero sexually engaged with someone else. But *Much Ado* once again steers us away from thinking of Platonic knowledge, and with it Platonic and Aristotelian models of mimetic performance, as the primary medium for dramatic action. In other words, it is not simply that one person (Margaret) has stood in for another (Hero), therefore deceiving Claudio in the manner Plato laments in *The Republic* and to which Aristotle accedes to in his *Poetics*.[19] Instead, what preoccupies these scenes is how Claudio disposes himself in preparation for what the truth may be. When Don John relays to Claudio and Don Pedro that Hero may be unfaithful, he frames the accusation in terms of Claudio's *reaction* to the news. After Claudio repeats Don John's accusation—"Disloyal?"—Don John clarifies: "Think you of a worse title, and I will fit her to it. Wonder not till further warrant" (3.2.97, 99–100). Even though no evidence has yet been proffered for any scandal, Claudio immediately prepares to humiliate Hero: "If I see anything tonight why I should not marry her, tomorrow in the congregation where I should wed, there will I shame her" (3.3.111–13). The scene ends with a burst of *stichomythia* that adds tragic portent to the scene, as if Hero's guilt has been overdetermined:

> DON PEDRO. O day untowardly turned!
> CLAUDIO. O mischief strangely thwarting!

---

[19] See Aristotle and Plato. For a critique of mimesis and gender, see Diamond.

DON JOHN. O plague right well prevented! So
will you say when you have seen the sequel.

(3.3.119–21)

With a hiss of sibilants, Don John exits the scene, a serpentine figure leaving
Don Pedro and Claudio to experience the Fall preemptively, before gaining
any real knowledge. They have already marked the day as "turned" by
thwarting them with mischief. Tellingly, and despite the intervention of
many directors, the actual scene of deception does not occur for us to
witness. The play blinks. We miss what should be a key deliberation on the
gullibility of Claudio and the deceptive prowess of Don John, Borachio,
and Margaret. Much like Hero's whispered profession of love, we are
denied knowledge and must judge instead without an appeal to the
"truth." Of course, we know what this truth is, but the play calls attention
to our ability to deduce this based upon our evaluations. As such, it realizes
in theatrical performance a goal of Stoic practice. Claudio, the bad pupil,
lifts himself out of the present and prepares himself for what he *will* do. He
loses the sense of critical indifference that would allow him to acclimate
himself to the here-and-now with the proper clinical sense of reason.

  The clearest example of the play utilizing Hero in a practice of Stoic
performance occurs with her feigned death. Imagining death fulfils a signal
exercise for the Stoic trainee. For Marcus Aurelius, waking every morning
with a reminder of the certainty of death helped his mind disengage from
the needless contingencies to which he could become overly attached. This
exercise utilizes a highly performative grammar, as Foucault notes:
"Meditating death is placing yourself, in thought, in the situation of someone who is in the process of dying, or who is about to die, or who is living
his last days . . . It is becoming, through thought, the person who is dying or
whose death is imminent" (*Hermeneutics* 358). The early modern era
absorbed the Stoic belief in a fundamental enmeshment of philosophy and
death, as evinced by the title alone of an early essay of Montaigne's, "That
to Philosophize is to Learn to Die." Montaigne, following the Stoics (and
other classical philosophers), suggests that death, in its unknowability,
cannot truly be feared; instead, we fear the trappings and ceremonies that
surround death. When stripped to its fundamental blankness, death gives us

a profound sameness, even community. "The advantage of life," as a result, "is not measured in length, but in use" (67).[20] To confront death in its simplicity relieves us of the hollow values we attach to it, and thus the task of philosophy is to "strip the mask from things as well as from persons; when it is off, we shall find beneath only that same death which a valet of a mere chambermaid passed through not long ago without fear" (68). As goes the chambermaid, so goes an emperor. The limpidity granted by meditating on death consoles us to focus on the present, on what we can control, not the *adiaphora* that saturate the suits and trappings that surround our end.

When the friar puts forth the plot to pretend that Hero has died, he invokes the structure of a Stoic exercise of imagining death, but he predicts a markedly non-Stoic pattern of behavior. Rather than have her death treated as a symptom of an unknowable cosmic force, one that may force us to evaluate how little of the external world we can control, the friar conscripts her as a pedagogical token, a prop to help Claudio realize her value and thus his culpability: "For so it falls out / That what we have we prize not to the worth / Whiles we enjoy it, but being lacked and lost, / Why, then we rack the value, then we find / The virtue that possession would not show us / Whiles it was ours" (4.1.217–22).[21] He is assured of this outcome—"doubt not but success"—but precisely the opposite result ensues. Claudio, with shocking immediacy, resumes his youthful flippancy, brought to the fore in a particularly jarring exchange with a deadly serious Benedick, who has followed Beatrice's imperative to "Kill Claudio" and challenged him to a duel. Claudio adheres to neither a Stoic plan of training his judgment nor the friar's hoped-for attachment to the violent

---

[20] For a treatment of Montaigne's engagement with Stoicism, which begins in the *Essays* as endorsement but, certainly by the time of Montaigne's long treatment of skepticism, "Apology for Raymond Sebond," takes on a more critical air, see Barbour and Sims.

[21] Berger Jr. similarly finds the friar's plan almost comically inept: "The friar's practice is a travesty on religious psychology, conversion, and ethical self-transformation" (313). For more on Stoicism's faith in an ordered world—and how that faith produces a capacity for chaos—see Sherman.

demonstration of *adiaphora*. Instead he indulges in what Benedick sums up as "gossip-like humor," and the scene of their confrontation brims with jarring tonal shifts between Benedick's gravity and the two gentlemen's attempts to joke with their former friend. It is not until he hears of Hero's innocence, brought to light by Dogberry's protracted investigation, that Claudio begins to mourn: "Sweet Hero! Now thy image doth appear / In the rare semblance that I loved it first" (5.1.241–42). When he then repents to Leonato, his careful language skirts pedantry: "Yet sinned I not / But in mistaking" (264–65). The intransitive verb "mistake" names here a misuse of *judgment*, not simply of mis-taking one thing for another; the OED defines this usage, contemporary to Shakespeare, as "to err in opinion or judgement." Claudio defines his error as possessing the incorrect disposition and drawing the wrong judgment, not of being fooled by the withholding of knowledge. He also "sees" Hero suddenly, placing value less on her quantifiable physical appearance but instead on how he has internally constructed her representation. He is "assenting to an appearance," as Nussbaum glosses Chrysippus (*Therapy* 374)—and by assenting to a specifically *inward* appearance, he echoes the exercises by which Marcus Aurelius and others would ensure themselves of their own reasonable capacity, by which that reason would be trained and honed. When Claudio attempts to stage his redemption, he does so by confirming his disposition, rather than relying on any empirical, observable appearances; his promise—cut from many productions, for obvious reasons—that he will "hold my mind were she an Ethiope" confirms, albeit with striking bigotry, that *his* new self distinguishes itself from the former version by giving itself over to whatever presents itself as new, in the moment (5.4.38).

There is something perverse in attempting to recover Claudio as a pupil who trains himself to recognize virtue with Stoic exercises. He is not a sage, but a rash, sexist, self-obsessed character who does not nearly reach enlightenment, much less sagacity. But the truly Stoic approach would be to recognize even Claudio's capacity for growth—*especially* his. Throughout the play, Shakespeare insists on language that favors judgment over knowledge, reason over truth, and inward cultivation over outward assurances. He centers this language in part on someone who seems barely redeemable; most critics have found him excessively and implausibly foolish.[22] But if we resituate our own criteria for evaluating Claudio outside of what we think we know about him and instead chart his own capacity to reason, his virtue, we find that *Much Ado* documents a radical performance practice plucked from antiquity and laundered through early modern social codes. In doing so the play challenges our *own* capacity to reason, and it can only do so through the embodied and performed interaction between it and us. We are not asked to sympathize and are kept at a distance from the proceedings, as cemented in Benedick's jarring final line, a schoolyard riposte aimed at Don Pedro: "Prince, thou art sad—get thee a wife, get thee a wife! / There is no staff more reverend than one tipped with horn" (5.4.120–21). This bizarre and obscure jape plays on cuckoldry imagery while suggesting that one's staff—wife?—may become "tipped" or "tupped" and thus gain a form of ironic reverence. Recalling Nussbaum's novel observation of Stoicism's Brechtian affinities, we can view the bawdiness of this line as a distancing device that ensures we do not overly invest ourselves in the fate of the personae on stage and instead commit to a response guided with "no more than reason." Sympathy would connote an attachment to the passions, to our judgments, rather than to our rational selves, and the humor the play exercises in this moment attempts to keep that rationality alive.

Rather than prompt Brecht's revolutionary response, in which the audience questions otherwise invisible social forces, what the play ultimately demands, then, is our indifference, figured as an audit of our own reason and thus our own capacity. In *Much Ado*'s deployment of wit, dazzling displays of creative reading and repurposing of idiom, persistent favoring of introspection over external investigation, and obstinate refusal of sympathy, indifference breaks free from the image of the unfeeling Stoic Leonato mocks in his faux passion. Rather, the indifferent spectator remains a highly theatrical one, removed from the lure of prediction or knowledge but attentive to the action on display. Indifference becomes not the lack of action but something that, like Castiglione's grace, demands rigorous curation: it is something to be

---

[22] Claudio has few fans (see Inchbald, Hays, Berger Jr.), though Craik attempts some recuperation.

practiced. The play aestheticizes this practice as theatre, and in this way, it makes good on its title and gives us nothing—not the nothing of infinity, nor the nothing of existential absence, but simply the "nothing" that brushes aside our investment in recovering the truth and asks us instead why we think we are even ready to receive it.

References

Aristotle. *The Poetics*. Translated by Hippocrates G. Apostle, Elizabeth A. Dobbs, and Morris A. Parslow. The Peripatetic Press, 1990.

Attridge, Harold. "An 'Emotional' Jesus and Stoic Tradition." *Stoicism in Early Christianity*, edited by Tuomas Rasimus, Troels Engberg-Pedersen, and Ismo Dunderberg. Baker, 2010, pp. 77–92.

Barbour, Reid. *English Epicures and Stoics: Ancient Legacies in Early Stuart Culture*. University of Massachusetts Press, 1998.

Beckwith, Sarah. *Shakespeare and the Grammar of Forgiveness*. Cornell University Press, 2012.

Behrent, Michael, and Daniel Zamora, editors. *Foucault and Neoliberalism*. Polity, 2016.

Berger Jr., Harry. "Against the Sink-a-Pace: Sexual and Family Politics in *Much Ado About Nothing*." *Shakespeare Quarterly*, vol. 33, no. 3, 1992, pp. 302–13.

Berry, Ralph. "Much Ado About Nothing: Structure and Texture." *English Studies*, vol. 52, no. 1–6, 1971, pp. 211–33.

Braden, Gordon. *Renaissance Tragedy and the Senecan Tradition: Anger's Privilege*. Yale University Press, 1985.

Brecht, Bertolt. "A Short Organum for the Theatre." *Brecht on Theatre: The Development of an Aesthetic*. Translated by John Willet. Farrar, Straus, and Giroux, 1964. 179–205

Campbell, Timothy, and Adam Sitze, editors. *Biopolitics: A Reader*. Duke University Press, 2013.

Castiglione, Baldassare. *The Book of the Courtier*, edited by Virginia Cox. Translated by Thomas Hoby. Everyman, 1994.

Cavell, Stanley. *Disowning Knowledge in Seven Plays of Shakespeare*. Cambridge University Press, 2003.

Pursuits of Happiness: The Hollywood Comedy of Remarriage. Harvard University Press, 1981.

Cicero (Marcus Tullius Cicero). *The Booke of Marcus Tullius Cicero entitled Paradoxa Stoicorum*. Translated by Thomas Newton. [T. Marsh], 1569.

    On the Ideal Orator (De Oratore). Translated by James M. May and Jakob Wisse. Oxford University Press, 2001.

Collington, Philip D. "'Stuffed with all Honourable Virtues': *Much Ado About Nothing* and *The Book of the Courtier*." *Studies in Philology*, vol. 103, no. 3, 2006, pp. 281–312.

Cook, Carol. "'The Sign and Semblance of Her Honor': Reading Gender Difference in *Much Ado About Nothing*." *PMLA*, vol. 101, no. 2, 1986, pp. 186–202.

Craik, T.W. "Much Ado About Nothing." *Scrutiny*, vol. 19, no. 4, 1953, pp. 297–316.

Dealy, Ross. *The Stoic Origins of Erasmus's Philosophy of Christ*. University of Toronto Press, 2017.

Diamond, Elin. *Unmaking Mimesis: Essays on Feminism and Theatre*. Routledge, 1997.

Epictetus. *Discourses*. Translated by George Long. D. Appleton and Company, 1904.

    The Handbook (The Enchiridion). Translated by Nicholas P. White. Hackett, 1983.

    The Manuell of Epictetus, Translated out of Greek and into French, and now into English. Translated by John Sanford. 1567.

    The Moral Philosophie of the Stoicks. Translated by Thomas James. 1598.

Eskew, Doug. "*Richard II* and the Unforgetting Messiah." *Exemplaria*, vol. 27, no. 4, 2015, pp. 307–28.

Fitzgerald, William. "The Epistolary Tradition." *The Oxford History of Classical Reception in English Literature, Volume 2 (1558–1660)*, edited by Patrick Cheney and Philip Hardie. Oxford University Press, 2015, pp. 273–90.

Foucault, Michel. "The Ethics of the Concern of the Self as a Practice of Freedom." Translated by P. Aranov and D. McGrawth. *The Essential Foucault: Selections from the Essential Works of Foucault, 1954–1984*, edited by Paul Rabinow and Nikolas Rose. The New Press, 1994, pp. 25–42.

   The Hermeneutics of the Subject: Lectures at the Collège de France 1981–1982, edited by Frédéric Gros. Translated by Graham Burchell. Picador, 2005.

   Subjectivity and Truth: Lectures at the Collège de France 1980–1981, edited by Frédéric Gros. Translated by Graham Burchell. Palgrave Macmillan, 2017.

Garber, Marjorie. *Shakespeare After All*. Anchor Books, 2004.

Goddard, Harold. "Much Ado About Nothing." *The Meaning of Shakespeare, Volume 1*. University of Chicago Press, 1951, pp. 271–80.

Gottlieb, Derek. *Skepticism and Belonging in Shakespeare's Comedy*. Routledge, 2016.

Greenblatt, Stephen. "*Much Ado About Nothing*." *The Norton Shakespeare*, edited by Greenblatt et al. Norton, 2016, pp. 337–45.

Grier, Miles. "Staging the Cherokee Othello: An Imperial Economy of Indian Watching." *The William and Mary Quarterly*, vol. 73, no. 1, 2016, pp. 73–106.

Guevara, Antonio de. *The Golden Boke of Marcus Aurelius*. Translated by John Bourchier Berners. [Thomas Berthelet], 1545.

Habermas, Jürgen. *The Philosophical Discourse of Modernity*. Translated by Frederick Lawrence. Polity, 1987.

Hadot, Pierre. *The Inner Citadel: The Meditations of Marcus Aurelius*. Translated by Michael Chase. Harvard University Press, 2001.

Philosophy as a Way of Life, edited by Arnold I. Davidson. Translated by Michael Chase. Blackwell, 1995.

Hays, Janice. "Those 'soft and delicate desires': *Much Ado* and the Distrust of Women." *The Woman's Part: Feminist Criticism of Shakespeare*, edited by Carolyn Ruth Swift Lenz, Gayle Greene, and Carol Thomas Neely. University of Illinois Press, 1983, pp. 79–99.

Helfer, Rebecca. "Wit and the Art of Memory in Nashe's *Unfortunate Traveler*." *English Literary Renaissance*, vol. 47, no. 3, 2017, pp. 325–54.

Henze, Richard. "Deception in Much Ado About Nothing." *Studies in English Literature, 1500–1900*, vol. 11, no. 2, 1971, pp. 187–201.

Homer. *The Iliad*. Translated by Robert Fitzgerald. Farrar, Straus, and Giroux, 1974.

Inchbald, Elizabeth. "Remarks." *The British Theatre, or, A Collection of Plays:* Much Ado About Nothing, *Vol. 13*. Hurst, Robinson, and Co., 1808, 2–5.

Irvine, William B. *A Guide to the Good Life: The Ancient Art of Stoic Joy*. Oxford University Press, 2009.

Jonson, Ben. "Bartholomew Faire." *The Alchemist and Other Plays*, edited by Gordon Campbell. Oxford University Press, 1995.

Kottman, Paul. "Memory, 'Mimesis,' Tragedy: The Scene before Philosophy." *Theatre Journal*, vol. 55, no. 1, 2003, pp. 81–97.

Kuzner, James. *Shakespeare as a Way of Life: Skeptical Practice and the Politics of Weakness*. Fordham University Press, 2016.

Leo, Russ. "Michel Foucault and Digger Politics." *Studies in English Literature, 1500–1900*, vol. 58, no. 1, 2018, pp. 169–94.

Lipsius, Justus. *Two Bookes of Constancie*. Translated by John Stradling. [Richard Johnes] 1595.

Lupton, Julia. *Citizen-Saints: Shakespeare and Political Theology*. The University of Chicago Press, 2005.

Mack, Peter. "The Classics in Humanism, Education, and Scholarship." *The Oxford History of Classical Reception in English Literature, Volume 2 (1558–1660)*, edited by Patrick Cheney and Philip Hardie. Oxford University Press, 2015, pp. 29–56.

McEachern, Claire. "Introduction." *Much Ado About Nothing*. Thomson Learning, 2006. 1–144.

Mezzatesta, Michael. "Marcus Aurelius, Fray Antonio de Guevara, and the Ideal of the Perfect Prince in the Sixteenth Century." *Art Bulletin*, vol. 60, 1984, pp. 620–33.

Miller, D.A. *The Novel and the Police*. University of California Press, 1989.

"mistake, v." *OED Online*, Oxford University Press, www.oed.com/view/Entry/120073. Accessed May 2, 2018.

Moi, Toril. *Revolution of the Ordinary: Literary Studies after Wittgenstein, Austin, and Cavell*. The University of Chicago Press, 2017.

Montaigne, Michel de. "That to Philosophize is to Learn to Die." *The Complete Essays of Montaigne*. Translated by Donald M. Frame. Stanford University Press, 1957, pp. 56–68.

Munro, Ian. "Shakespeare's Jestbook: Wit, Print, Performance." *ELH*, vol. 71, no. 1, 2004, pp. 89–113.

Nussbaum, Martha. "Poetry and the Passions: Two Stoic Views." *Passions and Perceptions: Studies in Hellenistic Philosophy of Mind*, edited by Jacques Brunschwig and Martha C. Nussbaum. Cambridge University Press, 1993, pp. 97–149.

    The Therapy of Desire: Theory and Practice in Hellenistic Ethics. Princeton University Press, 1994.

Plato. *The Republic*. Translated by C.D.C. Reeve. Hackett, 2004.

Richards, Jennifer. "Assumed Simplicity and the Critique of Nobility: Or, How Castiglione Read Cicero." *Renaissance Quarterly*, vol. 54, no. 2, 2001, pp. 460–84.

Rossiter, A.P. "Much Ado About Nothing." *Angel with Horns and Other Shakespeare Lectures*, edited by Graham Storey. Longmans, 1961, pp. 65–81.

Scott, Mary Augusta. "*The Book of the Courtyer:* A Possible Source of Benedick and Beatrice." *PMLA*, vol. 16, no. 4, 1901, pp. 475–502.

Seneca. *Letters on Ethics*. Translated by Margaret Graver and A.A. Long. University of Chicago Press, 2015.

Seneca. *The Works of Lucius Annaeus Seneca, both Morall and Naturall*. Translated by Thomas Lodge. 1614.

Schechner, Richard. *Performance Studies: An Introduction*. Routledge, 2002.

Shakespeare, William. *Hamlet*, edited by Harold Jenkins. Methuen & Co. Ltd., 1997 [1982].

   Much Ado About Nothing, edited by Claire McEachern. Thomson Learning, 2006.

Sherman, Donovan. "Embodied Stoicism in Marston's Antonio Plays." *English Literary Renaissance*, vol. 48, no. 3, 2018, pp. 291–313.

Sidney, Philip. "The Defence of Poesy." *The Major Works*, edited by Katherine Duncan-Jones. Oxford University Press, 2002, pp. 212–51.

Sims, Gregory. "Stoic Virtues/Stoic Vices: Montaigne's Pyrrhic Rhetoric." *Journal of Medieval and Early Modern Studies*, vol. 23, no. 2, 1993, pp. 235–66.

Sofer, Andrew. *Dark Matter: Invisibility in Drama, Theater, and Performance*. University of Michigan Press, 2013.

"stock, n.1 and adj." *OED Online*, Oxford University Press, www.oed.com /view/Entry/190595. Accessed May 2, 2018.

Taylor, Diana. *The Archive and the Repertoire: Performing Cultural Memory in the Americas*. Duke University Press, 2003.

Ulrici, Hermann. "Much Ado About Nothing—Taming of the Shrew." *Shakespeare's Dramatic Art and His Relation to Calderon and Goethe*. Chapman Brothers, 1846, pp. 289–99.

Cambridge Elements

Shakespeare Performance

W. B. Worthen
Barnard College

W. B. Worthen is Alice Brady Pels Professor in the Arts, and
Chair of the Theatre Department at Barnard College. He is also
co-chair of the Ph.D. Program in Theatre at Columbia
University, where he is Professor of English and Comparative
Literature.

ADVISORY BOARD

Pascale Aebischer *University of Exeter*

Todd Barnes Ramapo *College of New Jersey*

Susan Bennett *University of Calgary*

Gina Bloom *University of California, Davis*

Rustom Bharucha *Jawaharlal Nehru University, New Delhi*

Bridget Escolme *Queen Mary University of London*

Alan Galey *University of Toronto*

Douglas Lanier *University of New Hampshire*

Sonia Massai *King's College London*

Julia Reinhard Lupton *University of California, Irvine*

Peter W. Marx *University of Köln*

Alfredo Michel Modenessi, *National Autonomous University of Mexico*

Robert Shaughnessy *Guildford School of Acting, University of Surrey*

Ayanna Thompson *George Washington University*

Yong Li-Lan *National University of Singapore*

ABOUT THE SERIES

Shakespeare Performance is a dynamic collection in a field that is both always emerging and always evanescent. Responding to the global range of Shakespeare performance today, the series launches provocative, urgent criticism for researchers, graduate students and practitioners. Publishing scholarship with a direct bearing on the contemporary contexts of Shakespeare performance, it considers specific performances, material and social practices, ideological and cultural frameworks, emerging and significant artists and performance histories.

Cambridge Elements

Shakespeare Performance

CPSIA information can be obtained
at www.ICGtesting.com
Printed in the USA
LVHW040710180819
628035LV00002B/24

9 781108 707299